HOW TO LIVE (ALMOST) HAPPILY WITH A TEENAGER

Lois Leiderman Davitz, Ph.D.
Joel Robert Davitz, Ph.D.

Winston Press

Library of Congress Catalog Card Number: 81-52349
ISBN: 0-86683-624-1
Printed in the United States of America.
5 4 3 2
Winston Press, Inc.   430 Oak Grove   Minneapolis, MN 55403

Contents

Preface

Our sons came home for an unexpected visit from college. As a matter of routine they asked us how we were and what we were doing. Usually on these visits whether we told them our insurance rates had doubled, the hot water heater had burst, or the dishwasher had sprung a leak didn't matter very much; their response was "Great!" We never got much of a chance to go into details, but that didn't bother us. We understood. After all, from their perspective details about how two middle-aged adults muddled their way through twenty-four hours every day hardly measured up to the excitement in their lives, and this is what they usually wanted to discuss. However, on this particular visit, we were surprised.

"How's everything? What are you doing?"

"Writing a book for parents about how to raise adolescents."

"Great!" And then a few moments of stunned silence. "What did you say you were doing?"

"Working on a book for parents on how to get through adolescence."

"It's too late. They've been through adolescence."

"How to help their kids."

"You helped us?" The idea that we had helped them, or at least made an effort in that direction, obviously was a revelation.

"What did you think we were doing?"

"You really want to know?"

"Yes, we'd like to know. What did you think we were doing?"

"Nagging, mostly."

"That's all?"

"Getting in the way."

"What else?"

"Treated us like we were four years old sometimes."

"Like when?"

"Like telling us what to eat, where to go, you know what you did."

"All right. Tell us more."

"Well, Dad was always saying how when he was a kid he got on something like tennis and kept at it until he did well."

"Was that bad?"

"Not exactly bad, but we got the impression he felt we didn't do the same thing."

"Well, you didn't."

"That's exactly what we mean."

"What is exactly what you mean?"

"Criticize."

"It wasn't criticism," we defended ourselves. "We were helping."

"Whatever it was, it was a pain in the ass most of the time."

"Anything else?"

"You're writing the book, not us."

"We'd like to hear your ideas about how we were as parents. When you have kids, would you raise them the same way?"

"Yes and no."

"What's the yes part?"

"Cared, maybe that's it. You cared. In fact, you cared too damned much sometimes. There were times we would have given anything to escape, but there wasn't any place to hide. Maybe the closet."

They exchanged looks. Perhaps they were going too far.

Rather than continue the conversation in that direction, they turned the question back on us.

"How were we as adolescents?"

"Great!" was our immediate response. Even when the rock went through the front window during an outburst of anger. Great, even when we were told to _____ off. Great, even when a new tennis racket was thrown into a pond after another session of our helpful instruction. Great, even when we sat up half the night, heads in our hands, wondering if we could make it through adolescence. There were times when we were as bewildered as any parent could possibly be, when both of us desperately wished that we could somehow skip this stage in our children's lives. And yet, when we thought about this period of our lives, we realized that the kids were really great. We shared their problems, their worries, their conflicts; we did our share of nagging, had our share of stormy battles, and experienced the anxieties that most parents feel when their children leave home and face the world pretty much on their own. But their adolescence involved far more than problems, worries, and battles. Perhaps more than anything else it was a time when we shared the excitement of their growing up, the joy and satisfaction of seeing them develop from children into strong and psychologically healthy young adults.

In this book we want to share that learning. Our goal is

not to convert parents into all-understanding saints or to change adolescents into conforming robots. All of us have our human foibles, our special needs, our unique personalities, and there is no magic formula that can guarantee an entirely smooth transition from childhood to adult life. Nevertheless, there are rational principles of parenting that can help. We hope to make these principles clear in this book and thus help both parents and their teenagers make it through the dynamic years of adolescence with a sense of joy, satisfaction, and fulfillment.

Lois Leiderman Davitz, Ph.D.
Joel Robert Davitz, Ph.D.

Rational Parenting

Something more than tender loving care.

In a survey of over two hundred and fifty parents of adolescents from all over the United States and Canada, we asked the question, "What do you want most for your adolescents?" The answers we received varied a great deal, but the majority of responses fell into two major categories: happiness and achievement.

In the light of these results, our central question is this: How can adults help adolescents reach the two interrelated goals of happiness and achievement? By and large, adults who live and work with teenagers find that the tender loving care that was so crucial during a child's infancy and childhood is no longer enough when the child reaches adolescence. Of course, love, tender concern, and sympathetic understanding are necessary at all stages of life, but in helping adolescents gain a happy, achieving maturity, parents must do something more than offer tender loving care. This something more is *rational parenting*. It is not a matter of special technical knowledge, but rather a process involving certain human qualities.

True to Themselves

Rational parents are genuinely themselves in relation to their adolescents. There is no shame, no act, no double-talk. They don't presume to be perfect human beings, and they never play the role of the Perfect Parent. They have their problems, their worries, their personal idiosyncracies, their hopes and disappointments. They get angry and irritable, they are loving and happy, sometimes confused and depressed just like everyone else. But in relation to their adolescents they are honest, straightforward, authentic, and human. They are not always conventionally polite, and sometimes they say and do things that might surprise an outsider, but underlying their relationships with their adolescents is a sense of unshakeable mutual trust. As a result, regardless of whatever disagreements, arguments, conflicts they get into, their adolescents know that they can count on their parents not for a meaningless pat on the back or a conventional word of affection, but for a genuine human reaction.

Empathically in Touch

Rational parents are psychologically and empathically in touch with their adolescents. They don't spend much time analyzing the psychological why's and wherefore's of their adolescents' behavior, but more important, they can step into their adolescents' shoes, see the world as their adolescents see it. In seeking to understand their adolescents, they empathize rather than analyze. Even when they disagree with their adolescents (and sometimes the disagreements are loud and clear), they have the capacity to shift from their own points of view and get to a sense of the world from their adolescents' perspectives. This doesn't mean that they simply accept their adolescents' views. They experience the world "as if" they were adolescents, at the same time never forgetting they are adults and parents. While they can empathically understand their adolescents' experiences, they also see the world from their own perspectives as parents.

Listening and Hearing

Rational parents don't have trouble expressing their opinions, but they also have a talent for listening and hearing what their adolescents have to say. There is no magic in this talent; it comes down to simple skills like paying attention without interrupting, without prejudging what is said, and without trying to out-guess or out-wit their adolescents. They're not out to make "points" in some pseudo-game of parenting, and in their arguments they don't fall into the role of prosecuting attorney. They sometimes get into battles with their adolescents, but there is a give-and-take in these battles, a sharing of experiences, without one person trying to prove the other guilty.

Owning Feelings

Rational parents talk *with*, not *at*, their adolescents, and in the give-and-take of their discussions they freely and openly express their feelings. But in expressing these feelings, they clearly own these feelings themselves. Thus, when they're angry, they honestly say "I am angry," without foisting the blame on their adolescents. In expressing their feelings, they don't use indirect *You-messages*, such as "You are at fault," "You are bad," or "You are wrong." They stick to simple, direct, and honest *I-messages*: "I am angry," "I am tired," "I am confused," "I am afraid"—messages that clearly indicate that these are the parents' own feelings, not projections onto their adolescents. Because these parents own up to their own feelings and express them directly without projecting the blame onto someone else, their adolescents can deal with these feelings instead of defending themselves against parental attacks.

Focusing on the Problem at Hand

When rational parents and their adolescents disagree, they confront the differences without trying to hide them in the family closet. It's not just a matter of tolerating differences, but a genuine acceptance of the fact that from time to time human beings are bound to differ with one another. Moreover, these parents stick to the particular problem at hand without generalizing to everything else. Their relationships with their adolescents are by no means always smooth and filled with sunshine. Like all other parents they go through periods of stress and are sometimes very confused and don't really know what to do. But they are able to face these problems with their adolescents and keep their concern focused on the immediate issues. In this respect, then, they are down-to-earth, practical, and concrete, dealing with each issue as it arises without trying to resolve at once all the problems of human development.

Willing to Risk

Rational parents are willing to take a reasonable chance on their adolescents' growing maturity. This willingness isn't based on blind faith or an unrealistic view of the world. They are aware of the real dangers in the world, the risks inevitable in all human development. But they trust their adolescents' abilities to face the normal stresses of growing up. They realize that growing up can never be cut-and-dried according to some pre-established plan. Every human being has his or her own unique pattern of development, and there is no single solution to any problem that fits everyone. Thus, rational parenting always involves some risk that the choices taken, the decisions made, may not turn out to be the best of all possible choices in the long run. But more important than almost any specific decision is the parents' trust in their adolescents' capacity to make choices and thus gain the freedom to grow.

Respecting Independence

Although rational parents have a close and continuing relationship with their adolescents, they also have a profound respect for each individual's independence—both their own and that of their adolescents. These parents lead a major part of their lives independent from their adolescents, and many of their most important satisfactions in life have little or nothing to do with their adolescents. They are deeply committed to the everyday responsibilities of parenting, but they do not feel that they are sacrificing, or that they should sacrifice, other significant values in an attempt to live for the sake of their children. They are not always psychologically available. Sometimes they just feel like withdrawing from their adolescents, and when this happens, they don't fake the role of an interested parent. But as a result of this self-respect for their own individuality and independence, they can be genuinely *there* when their adolescents really need them.

Similarly, rational parents respect their adolescents' need for privacy, individuality, and independence. They fully appreciate the fact that no matter how close and loving the relationship between parent and teenager, each has different needs, different interests, different activities, and to some extent live in different worlds. Rational parents value these differences, recognizing that they are an important aspect of the adolescent's development as a maturing individual.

Rational Parenting in Everyday Life

Rational parenting is not merely a set of characteristics; it is a *process* that must be incorporated into everyday living with adolescents. Rational parents don't put on a guise of rational parenting when a problem occurs, and then take it off when life is once again smooth. Rather, the give-and-take, the sharing of realities, the active encouragement and respect for individuality—the entire process of rational parenting— must become an intrinsic part of daily living.

Guidelines for Rational Parenting
1. Know yourself as a parent and be true to yourself.
2. Get in touch with how your adolescent experiences his or her world. In seeking to understand your adolescent, empathize, don't analyze.
3. Make a commitment to listening without interrupting, without prejudging, without trying to manipulate or out-wit your adolescent.
4. Stop the blame game with your adolescent. Remember that in parenting no one profits from proving someone else is guilty.
5. Express your feelings openly and honestly, but own your own feelings—don't project the blame for your own feelings onto your adolescent.
6. Confront the problems, conflicts, and disagreements you run into with your adolescent; don't ignore prob-

lems, hoping that they will take care of themselves.

7. Keep your eye on the problem at hand. Particularize, don't generalize. In dealing with the problems you and your adolescent face, be specific, practical, down-to-earth.

8. Be willing to take a reasonable chance on your adolescent's growing maturity.

9. Value the differences between you and your adolescent, and do whatever you can to encourage and reinforce your adolescent's independence and individuality. At the same time, remember to respect your own individuality and independence.

10. Make the process of rational parenting an intrinsic part of your everyday living.

Wasting Time

*Stop worrying about your teenager wasting time;
instead, examine your own attitudes about
work and make sure your adolescent knows
what you expect.*

We came home from the university after a hectic day over-filled with meetings, classes, appointments, telephone calls, memos that had to be written, letters to answer, students clamoring for attention—and not enough time to finish even half of what needed to be done. We had rushed home through traffic, and we planned to hurry through dinner so we could squeeze in some extra time working that evening. There just wasn't enough time in the day to do everything that had to be done, and we burst into the house like two steam engines going at full speed.

There was our teenage son sitting peacefully in the living room, feet up on a footstool, eyes closed, and a contented smile on his face.

"What have you been doing?" we asked.

"Sitting here. Why?" he answered.

"And the past hour? What have you been doing?"

"I don't know how long I've been here."

"What time did you get home from school?"

"I didn't look."

That fact alone was enough to shock us. One automatically looks at the clock when one gets home from work. One mentally makes out schedules to fill the remaining hours of the day. Our son had violated one of the rituals of adult life—checking the time and filling it to good purpose.

"What's the problem?" he asked. "Can't I just sit here?"

"Don't you have anything to do? You could at least take out the garbage. The car needs washing. The lawn mower needs cleaning." We bombarded him with a list of valuable, useful, time-consuming activities. We worried that he was just wasting time.

Parents waste an extraordinary amount of time worrying about their adolescents wasting time. "I don't know how my daughter can stand around doing nothing," complained one mother. "She and her friends will be out on the corner near our house for hours. I told her if she spent that same time doing something useful she'd be a lot better off."

Keeping busy in one way or another is a virtue in our culture. From the point of view of many adults, being cavalier about the use of time is immoral.

"He can lie in bed, hands behind his head, and do nothing for hours. With all the things he has to do, he can spend more time doing nothing than anyone I know."

A teenager doing nothing worries adults. Teenagers who stare too long or too frequently out of a classroom window soon discover their seats are changed so they won't be tempted to waste time "just looking." Adolescents discovered by parents merely sitting around doing nothing are likely to find a garden rake thrust into their hands or to be reminded of some chore that needs doing. Parents can be remarkably resourceful in dredging up lists of things to do whenever they discover their youngsters sneaking in a few precious hours of "nothingness."

We have served as mediators in countless arguments between parents and teenagers revolving around the issue of wasting time, and these arguments are rarely easy to resolve.

In our experience, both teenagers and their parents have legitimate points to make in these arguments, but it's difficult for each to see the other's point of view.

From an adolescent's perspective, what parents may call "wasting time" is clearly not a waste. Although they usually cannot explain why the various activities lumped under the general category of "wasteful" are in fact worthwhile, teenagers often sense the significant psychological purposes these activities serve.

For example, parents may complain that their teenagers spend too much time daydreaming instead of doing something useful. Yet, fantasy has several important functions in a teenager's development. In their daydreams, adolescents may try out various goals in the process of discovering the direction they want to take in their adult lives. Via fantasy, they can "live out" various possibilities, imagining what their lives would be like if they chose to pursue one line of work or another. Parents often worry that daydreaming will reduce the adolescent's motivation to achieve in the real world, but we have found that among teenagers, fantasies can operate in the opposite way. Daydreaming may increase, rather than decrease, achievement motivation.

One young woman, currently in her first year of medical school, admitted that her early teenage fantasies had been the principal factor behind her present career choice. Early in her teens she recalled spending considerable time thinking about becoming a doctor. A biography, a TV show, or a movie would "set her off," and she would imagine herself in the role of a "savior." She added, "When you're fifteen and someone asks you what you're daydreaming about, you'd sound silly if you told them you were doing some kind of lifesaving act." But in her fantasy life she felt safe enough to dream about saving people's lives; in a very important sense, she was rehearsing her later decision to become a doctor.

A colleague of ours, currently a respected chemistry professor, attributes his success to the inspiration given him by a recurrent fantasy that started in his teens. He recalled a science teacher in high school who insisted that all students wear laboratory coats in chemistry lab. The white coat became a symbol of professionalism, and our colleague reported that he vividly remembers the impression the symbol made on his mind as a fifteen-year-old.

While walking to school or at odd times during the day or before he went to sleep, he began to weave a whole picture of himself in adult life. The white coat, the laboratory, a series of complicated equipment—all part of his mental picture. He wryly noted that he never pushed himself too far in his fantasy, never really explored the purpose of the research or how the elaborate equipment worked. At the time, it was enough for him to imagine himself the head of an immense laboratory, handing out directives to assistants and making great discoveries. It was a daydream that he had over and over again, and he felt that it was an important part of his motivation for becoming a scientist. He compared himself to the adolescent who dreams of becoming a writer but isn't bogged down in fantasy by thinking about the work of writing, or the teenager who dreams of going on the stage but in fantasy doesn't have to worry about the work of learning lines. He felt his fantasy gave him a sense of excitement and a feeling of being special. The inevitable tedium that he endured through college and graduate school, the hours of drudgery that his vocation required, were softened by his recurrent fantasy of future success.

Remember that an adolescent's daydreams can serve important purposes. They can increase motivation. They also give adolescents a chance to "try out" various

behaviors in their imagination, without facing the
hazards of the real world.

Parents encourage little children to play "let's pretend"
games. It's good for the imagination when a five-year-old
sits in a paper carton and "drives" the carton down a race-
way to first place. It's creative thinking when a four-year-old
plays a budding chemist stirring a beaker of muddy water to
concoct a magic potion. Daydreaming in adolescents, however, scares a parent. We perhaps forget our own adolescent
dreams of being famous athletes, rock stars, scientists, presi-
dents, or whatever imaginative flight we dared to take.

Teenagers also use daydreams to "practice" their reactions
to future situations that concern them. These kinds of re-
hearsals in fantasy can serve to make new situations less
strange. One teenager of our acquaintance applied for a
summer job and was given an appointment for an interview.
He had never had steady employment nor had he even had a
job interview. The idea threw him into a panic. For a week
before the interview he couldn't stop imagining what was
going to happen. First, he pictured the interviewer as an
ogre who put him on the defensive. He fantasized the kinds
of questions he would be asked and devised appropriate
answers. Rejecting the ogre image, he then imagined a kind-
ly sort of interviewer and thought of any number of brilliant
responses to questions. By the time he actually went to the
interview, he said he felt like an "old hand."

We are not suggesting that all teenage daydreams serve
important developmental purposes. Many daydreams are
simply ways of temporarily escaping the stresses of everyday
life, which certainly has some psychological value for the
adolescent without any long-term implications. In any
event, whether fantasies have some immediate escape and
tension-reduction value or have longer-range benefits, the

time adolescents spend daydreaming is frequently not the waste that parents might believe it to be.

Don't be misled by the apparently pointless, rambling conversations teenagers have among themselves. Even though you may not be aware of it, these seemingly idle conversations are one of the chief ways in which adolescents check out their worlds and gain a realistic view of themselves and of others.

Parents sometimes complain to us about the rambling conversations teenagers have with one another—frequently over the telephone. The conversations seem to go 'round and 'round without making too much sense, and parents wonder why their teenager spends so much time "saying nothing," rather than finishing homework or doing something else worthwhile. The pointlessness, however, is more often apparent than real. In these conversations that appear to be going nowhere, adolescents are frequently checking out their perceptions of the world with other adolescents, testing their own views and interpretations against those of their peers.

On one occasion it took three hours for one of our teenagers to reach a decision not to take the car one particularly stormy night. As far as we were concerned, the decision should have taken five minutes. One look out the window was enough to see that the roads were impassable. However, the decision for him was one that could only be reached after endless discussions with friends about the evening's plans. Each friend had an opinion; the back and forth exchanges were an important part of the decision process. Psychologists call this process "consensual validation," and it is a major way in which adolescents share their views of the world, their reactions to that world, and thus establish their sense of shared reality.

Adults should not be misled by the idling, apparently haphazard style of these interactions. It is precisely this tone of uninvolvement, inactivity, triviality which permits adolescents to share their reactions with one another in a safe, non-threatening atmosphere, and by sharing gain a fuller perspective on themselves and the world in which they live.

Thus, much of what some parents consider "wasting time" is in fact a very meaningful part of the process of growing up. Parents, nevertheless, have a valid point in their complaints. The central problem is not really wasting time, but rather the recognition that any kind of achievement requires work—and parents may be concerned that their adolescents do not fully appreciate this fundamental fact of life. Complaints about wasting time, therefore, are usually a cover for an underlying fear that an adolescent is not prepared to do the work necessary for achievement.

Worries about wasting time are so pervasive that we are convinced it represents a cultural phenomenon rather than a *problem* of particular families. The problem does not begin with adolescence. It derives, in part, from our attitudes toward work in childhood. In Western civilization childhood is associated with play and learning, and adulthood is associated with work. Children are expected to go to school and then to spend much of the rest of the time at play. Adults, on the other hand, are expected to work.

Adolescents are in-between, and parents are often not sure about what they should expect of their teenagers. Should the emphasis continue to be on learning and play, or should there be greater emphasis on work? The process of shifting from expectations appropriate for childhood to expectations appropriate for adulthood is not clear, and because of this lack of clarity, parents feel uncomfortable about the demands or lack of demands they make on their adolescents. Parents feel guilty about requiring their adolescents to work, and yet they also worry that without the experience of working, their adolescents will never learn to work. As a consequence of this discomfort, parents complain about their adolescents wasting time.

When it comes to the issue of work, make sure you are clear about your own expectations. What kind of work do you expect your adolescent to do? How much work do you expect? What do you think is the right balance of work and recreation for your adolescent? Clarify for yourself the answers to these questions, and once you are clear about your own expectations, be sure you are clear and consistent in conveying what you expect to your adolescents.

No one can tell parents exactly what to expect from their adolescents at any particular time. There is no single schedule of transition from child-like to more adult-like status that fits every adolescent, every parent, every situation. We cannot say that when an adolescent is fifteen every parent should expect a specific amount of work and that at sixteen this amount should be increased by so many percent. But we urge parents to clarify this issue for themselves and to be consistent in the stance they take with regard to working. Instead of bickering and arguing about their adolescents wasting time, parents might profitably examine their own attitudes to gain a clearer awareness of what they expect, and then, on the basis of this greater self-understanding, make sure their teenagers know what is expected of them.

When parents are clear and consistent in their expectations, when they know what they expect of their adolescent and clearly convey their expectations, there is very little problem about wasting time. Adolescents may agree or disagree with their parents' views, but it is a matter that can

be discussed, even argued, and eventually worked out in
day-to-day life. There is no need to bicker about a cover issue
such as wasting time.

Guidelines for Rational Parenting

If you are concerned about your adolescent wasting time, try
this:

Think about what your adolescent did this week. What
did your adolescent do that you feel was a waste of time? In
your opinion did your adolescent spend too much time
watching television? Listening to music? Talking on the
phone? Just hanging around doing nothing? Daydreaming?
Be specific in the ways you think your adolescent wasted
time during the past week.

Now, think about exactly how much time was wasted.
Was it a few minutes? A few hours? A day or more this
week? Why do you think it was a waste? What other things
might your adolescent have been doing that you feel would
have been better?

After you have clarified your own thoughts about this
issue, talk it over with your adolescent. Express your own
views clearly and explicitly, but be sure to be specific and
concrete about what happened this week. Don't generalize
to other times, and don't accuse your adolescent of being
lazy, neglectful, or any other general trait. Talk about specific
traits, not general ones.

Then *listen* to your adolescent's reaction and try to empathetically understand the way your adolescent experiences
what you think of as a waste of time. What meaning do
these activities have for your adolescent? At this point,
perhaps you will disagree with what your adolescent says,
but don't argue about it. You and your adolescent don't
have to agree all the time, but you do have to agree to live

peaceably with your disagreements. Don't try to force some artificial solution to your disagreements. If you can both understand each other's point of view, you will be well on your way to learning to live with your disagreements and to accepting the fact that each of you has a right to his or her own point of view without trying to impose that view on the other person.

Comparisons

Never compare your adolescent to other adolescents or to yourself as an adolescent.

Friends showed us the basement of their home, which their teenage son had converted into a finished recreation room. In one corner was a hi-fi set built by the same boy. In another corner was a completely equipped darkroom for developing and printing films, again the result of their son's efforts. Our admiration was unreserved. In our house we paid for film to be developed; we bought already assembled hi-fi units. Tinkering with the set involved little more than twisting on and off dials. That evening our family's dinner table conversation consisted of a recital of this adolescent's accomplishments. We were honestly praising. Our son agreed that his friend had considerable engineering and mechanical talents.

"Why don't you do something like that?" we asked. "Why spend money on film? If you like your camera so much, why not learn how to develop film? Why don't you do something with our basement?" Fantasies of money we could save, as well as the creativity involved, swept through our minds. Our son was silent. Suddenly he flung down his fork, got up from the table, and quietly said to us, "Do you feel stuck with me?"

Without realizing it, we had slipped into that most unfortunate of all child rearing errors—*parenting-by-comparison.* Our son's remark brought us face to face with what was really going on. We were making him feel inferior through the comparison. If we had wanted him to build a hi-fi set, we

should have come right to the point rather than beat around
the bush with the indirect criticism implied by our comparison of him with another teenager. Openly and directly expressing dissatisfaction is the only reasonable way to achieve
the goals a parent wants to achieve.

This is exactly what happened with one adolescent girl
whose mother had been trying to get her to lose weight. In
an effort to spur her daughter to diet, the mother repeatedly
brought up examples of other girls her daughter's age who
had lost weight and "looked so beautiful." The mother
thought the success stories would encourage her daughter to
do the same. However, when all the success stories were
about girls in the same school, the effect of the comparisons
was to drive the daughter to take another cookie from the
cookie jar.

*Whenever you parent-by-comparison, remember you
are sending the message "You are inferior."*

An adolescent can deal with a parent's honest criticism,
but it is virtually impossible for an adolescent to respond effectively to a comparison that implicitly carries the message
"You are inferior." That is the message your adolescent is
getting when you make these comparisons.

One parent told us that it was unrealistic to protect
adolescents from comparisons. According to this parent,
"sooner or later they have to know where they stand." But
when it comes to comparison, the important issue is not
whether a parent is being realistic or unrealistic. What
counts is the underlying message that the adolescent gets
from the parent. For the adolescent, it is this message that is
the most significant reality.

Furthermore, adolescents don't really need these parental
comparisons to learn where they stand in the world. Studies
show that youngsters are quite capable of identifying the

talents and accomplishments of their classmates. The competitive world outside provides plenty of feedback about one's own worth. The adolescent deserves the right to a first-rank position in his or her own family, and no adolescent ever needs to hear from a parent the message "You are not as good as someone else."

Instead of comparing one adolescent to another, emphasize the unique talents, the unique abilities, the individuality of your teenager.

Comparing one's adolescents to teenagers outside the immediate family is only one of the comparison games parents may play. In families with more than one child, comparisons between children may become part of the routine of daily life. In discussing this problem in her own family, one mother told us that she tried to avoid comparisons but somehow found herself saying things like "Why can't you get as good grades as your sister?" In this case, one child walked away regularly with school honors; the other didn't capture any prizes. But comparing their accomplishments didn't change the situation. Realizing this, the mother began to focus instead on the unique qualities of each child. One youngster excelled in writing; the other in sports. By focusing on the special qualities of each child, this mother was able to recognize and prize the individuality of her children. Rather than dwell on the fact that one child wasn't as successful as the other in academic matters, she learned to accept and appreciate each child as a unique and special individual.

Above all, keep yourself out of any comparisons.

In many instances of parenting-by-comparison, parents hold themselves up as idealized figures. One adolescent boy said he always knew when he was going to be in for a lecture on his behavior. His father would ask him into his study and

the opening phrase "When I was your age . . . " served
to introduce a list of his father's own remembered virtues
and his son's deficiencies.

The "Why can't you be like me?" stories, reported one
adolescent, made her feel angry and hopeless. In this case
the girl's mother was a well-known portrait artist; her father
a national television figure. Both parents had achieved success relatively early in life. "Just because I'm not interested
in what they're interested in, they call me lazy. I'm not lazy.
Their bag isn't my bag. They can't see this. They keep
pushing me to get excited about things that excite them.
Mom'll say, 'When I was your age, I was doing this,' and
she'll list the things. My dad does the same."

It's sometimes rough for parents to understand their
adolescents who stylistically seem quite different from either
of them. It always puzzled us, for example, that our adolescents couldn't see any virtue in having a regular Saturday job
during high school. We had gone to great lengths to impress
upon them the virtue of working every Saturday as the best
way to learn maturity and responsibility. They considered
sleeping late on Saturday mornings virtuous. We seized the
many opportunities to tell them about how hardworking,
mature, and responsible we were as adolescents—and how
we overcame seemingly insurmountable odds to become
such wonderful teenagers. We got a certain kick out of telling these stories until we realized that we were only making
life harder for them. They had to deal with the reality of
their todays, not the myths of our yesterdays.

*If you are angry or dissatisfied with your teenager, ex-
press your feelings openly and honestly. Don't hide
behind the pseudo-benign mask of parenting-by-
comparison.*

Comparing what we as parents were to the way our

teenagers are today is often a way of venting our anger while appearing to be benign parental figures concerned only with our child's growth and maturity. "After all," the comparing parent might argue, "I'm only pointing out what I did so my teenager will have a goal to shoot at." But of course that's nonsense. By and large, when we make these comparisons, we are not really trying to set goals or provide models for imitation; we are angry and dissatisfied, and by whatever comparisons we make, we are saying to our adolescent, "You are inferior."

This is the message that comes across loud and clear to the adolescent whenever the parent engages in *parenting-by-comparison*. It is not at all remarkable, therefore, that teenagers rarely greet such comparisons with their peers or stories about their parents' sterling adolescence with enthusiastic interest. The adolescents hear the implicit, unspoken message about their own inadequacies, and as one might reasonably expect, they become defensive and increasingly resistant to change.

Thus, the aim of helping adolescents overcome whatever problems they may be having is inevitably frustrated by parental comparison. A parent's anger may be temporarily alleviated by the indirect expression of aggression implicit in comparing the inadequacy of one's own teenager with the perfection of someone else, but in the long run this maneuver is bound to be self-defeating. If you're worried about your daughter's failure to work hard in school, regaling her with your own high school success (real or imagined) will only assure her continuing neglect of school work. If you're worried about your son's apparent lack of ambition, comparing him with some teenage paragon of achievement will only block any spark of motivation he might have. So cut out the comparisons with other teenagers and forget the stories about your own remarkable adolescence. Regardless of how true (or false) those stories might be, they only get in the way of your teenager's development—and add to your own parental frustrations.

If you are worried about your daughter's obvious lack of work in school, tell her what you're worried about directly, clearly, and without beating around the bush. If you are concerned about your son's seeming lack of ambition, share your concern with him openly and honestly. Teenagers, like everyone else, find it very hard to deal reasonably with indirect criticism implied by comparison. All of us can respond much more effectively and rationally to direct and honest criticism.

Guidelines for Rational Parenting
In talking with your adolescent during the past few weeks, have you made some direct or indirect comparison with another teenager? If you have, think about why you might have done it. Was it a way of expressing your dissatisfaction? Did the comparison imply some criticism of your adolescent?

How did your adolescent react? Did he or she welcome the comparison and share your views? Or did your adolescent interpret the comparison as an attack and react defensively?

Consider how you might feel if your adolescent were to compare you unfavorably to another parent. Do you think that you might feel it's an attack and thus react defensively?

The next time you feel the impulse to compare your adolescent to anyone else, stop a moment and think about the message you are conveying. Is the implied message "I think you are inferior to someone else"?

Rather than make such a comparison, clarify for yourself

what you are dissatisfied about. Then state your dissatisfaction openly and honestly. Be sure to own up to your own feelings of dissatisfaction. Remember, your feelings are the reality you experience, so share this reality with your adolescent directly. If you feel uncomfortable, tense, or angry, say so rather than hide these feelings behind a comparison.

Nagging

Stop nagging.

A number of years ago, when one of our sons was about sixteen, he received a tape recorder as a birthday gift. For the most part, the recorder was used to tape favorite records and his own singing and guitar playing. On one occasion, without our awareness, he taped all the dialogue that went on between the three of us. At that time we had been going through some stormy periods. He had been accusing us of nagging. In his words, "Lay off. I can't take it. Stop the damned nagging."

"Absurd," we told him. We offer advice, suggestions, helpful comments in our efforts to guide his development. Nag? Us nag? Impossible. We dismissed his accusations as a total lack of understanding and appreciation of what we were trying to do as good, concerned parents. Nagging is crude. As psychologists we would hardly stoop to such a practice.

His response was to pull out the tape recorder and ask us to listen to some tapes at our leisure. He told us that he had selected typical days to record—ordinary school days, before he left for school, after dinner, and just before bedtime. We offer a small verbatim sample of some of our two days of helpful parental guidance.

"Mickey, you better get up, kid. You're going to be late."

"Mickey, we called you once already. Daddy is going to be leaving and you're not even out of bed."

"Hey boy, I can't wait around for you. You better hurry.

By the way where did you put the car keys? I told you to leave them in the glove compartment.''

"Don't wear that shirt. There are buttons off. I'll put them on later. Why that shirt? You have ten shirts with buttons in your closet, and you choose one without buttons.''

"Mickey, you left your bite plate on the kitchen table. I told you that damn bite plate on the table makes me sick. Can't you put it in the box? Didn't the dentist give you a box?''

"You should remember to stop and get a new notebook. I noticed your notebook is ripped. You're going to lose all your papers.''

"Don't tell us you're remembering to put on acne medicine. We went out and spent a lot of money. The tube doesn't look like you've used it. It's for your own good. It's your face.''

"If I were you, I'd get a haircut. Why don't you stop after school. I can make an appointment for you.''

"Would you remember to take your laundry down to the basement before you go out. Laundry can't get done sitting in a basket in your room.''

"Those records are expensive. It's really wrong of you to leave them on the floor where they can get stepped on. If you had earned the money to buy them, you probably would take better care of your things.''

"Look at your jacket. Can't you hang it up *once?*''

"Are you going to be on the telephone much longer? I really do have to make a call.''

Listening was embarrassing. We rationalized. We didn't sound harsh and cruel. Take the comment about the records. The records were on the floor. They could get stepped on and ruined. He was proud of his record collection. We were only being helpful in reminding him the records could get stepped on. He should be thankful we were concerned about his records.

And the jacket. It was an expensive jacket. He had worn it the previous evening and hadn't hung it up. It was in a heap on the floor. We were just trying to teach him the value of money in relationship to purchases. All our intentions were motivated by righteous goodness.

Even the matter of getting up. He tended to oversleep, and he would get into trouble if he consistently came late to school. There was no question that our every comment was motivated by good intentions. For example, the bite plate issue. He did forget and could be in situations where people could justifiably take offense at having a pink plastic mouthpiece with attached wires sitting in the middle of a plate on a dinner table.

Despite our rationalizations and defenses, the tape's content revealed a constant barrage of "reminders." When we recovered from our initial chagrined reactions, we had to admit he had a point. In fact, probably more than fifty percent of all our disagreements stemmed from our nagging. We suspect this is true with many parents and their teenage children.

To stop your nagging, you must first become conscious of what you nag about and what triggers your nagging behavior.

Like any other bad habit that we wish to break, the first step is to become aware of it. In our case, our son's recording had been successful. At least we were made aware of what was happening. The next task was to find out what situations or circumstances started our chain of nags. The best person to help us accomplish this task was our son. We waited for a time when relations were calm and peaceful and then worked together to specify as precisely as we could the most frequent habitual nags and the circumstances that evoked that behavior. We had him write down all the things he thought we nagged him about. There were nags about haircuts, work, dirty jeans, loud music, late hours—seemingly trivial matters that were mentioned time and time again. Asking your teenager to write down all the nags and accepting the list without trying to defend yourself can go a long way toward curbing the nagging impulse most parents seem to possess.

In all fairness to ourselves and to other parents, the motivation to nag is benign, and most of us feel that one little reminder can't really do any harm—and might do some good. We are often so caught up in trying to help our adolescents grow up as we think they should that we forget the unfortunate consequences of our earlier nags. Thus, time and again we are trapped in the vicious circle of bickering that frequently begins with "Brush your teeth," "Do your homework," or "Change your clothes."

To help curb your nagging, every time you feel the impulse to nag, begin your comment with the phrase, "I don't trust you." This will remind you what you are actually communicating.

By and large, most parents when they look at the lists their adolescents draw up will discover that none of the issues in and of themselves is very important. Parents can reasonably wonder, if the nags are so inconsequential, why did our son—and why do most adolescents—react with so much anger? We feel it's not the nag itself that is so disturbing. Rather, it is the lack of trust in the message of the parental nag. When parents are about to nag, they can sometimes control their nagging behavior by actually saying "I don't trust you" before commenting about any of the minor problems they have mentioned to their adolescent repeatedly.

Thus, if a parent says "I don't trust you, have you done your homework?" or "I don't trust you, are you coming in late again tonight?" we can appreciate the message an adolescent gets from a parental nag.

For the adolescent, the message conveying a parent's lack of trust is by far the *loudest* part of any nag. It is a low blow to the adolescent, for it strikes at exactly the weakest point of the teenage ego—self-confidence. Despite their sometimes noisy bravado, adolescence almost by definition is a stage of development in which the individual is bound to be plagued by periods of self-doubt. This is only to be expected. There are enormous changes going on within the adolescent, both physical and psychological, and new challenges in all aspects of living are part of the teenager's everyday life. It is precisely because of these changes and challenges that adolescence is a period of such dramatic growth. And the normal price for intense psychological change is a certain lack of sureness, some self-doubt, and at least temporary loss of self-confidence. "Am I smart enough, good enough, to become the adult I want to become?" These are very real and undeniably serious concerns that every adolescent at one time or another suffers through, and it is little wonder, then, that adolescents are often not sure about trusting themselves.

Now, add to this image of normal teenage development the voice of a parent repeatedly and insistently crying, "I don't trust you." Of course those aren't the actual words spoken; the actual words are usually about homework, haircuts, clothes, or any of the other trivial issues that comprise the subject matter of the vast majority of nags. But the actual words spoken are far less important than the obvious, though implicit, messsage, "I don't trust you," that comes across loud and clear.

It is not at all surprising, therefore, to find that the adolescent's response to most nags is either a defensive withdrawal or a defensive attack—and rarely compliance with the manifest intent of the nag. The adolescent becomes sullenly withdrawn or angrily argumentative; the parent, in turn, becomes increasingly irritated; and before long, a vicious cycle is joined, and both parent and adolescent are caught up in another one of the painful battles that may punctuate the lives of teenagers and their families.

When you've identified what you nag about, make a distinction between what's good for your adolescent and what's good for you.

Although most parents sincerely believe that most of the nagging they do is for their youngster's own good, another motivating factor behind parental nagging has to do with the parent's own self-esteem. For example, at one point one of our youngsters was in the stage of wearing torn jeans, an equally disheveled T-shirt, sandals, and mismatched socks. We were "up the wall." We couldn't stand his appearance, and with sly remarks and reminders we kept after him on a daily basis. We even went so far as to sneak the torn jeans out of his room and throw them away. He rescued them before the garbage was collected. Why were we driven to nagging him about his dress? As he said, he didn't tell us what to wear; he was wearing the clothes and liked them. What difference did *his* old clothes make in our lives?

Why did we care? We were embarrassed by his appearance. We worried about the impression he made on the "outside world." His style of dress hardly permitted parental pride. Like many parents, we wanted to point to a neatly dressed adolescent and be able to say "This is our son." As it was, sometimes we wanted to hide. The reasons then for the nags not only were a concern about him but also a selfish concern for our own feelings. Although he didn't particularly approve or understand why we were so self-conscious, once we explained our embarrassment, he was willing to "help us out." A bargain was struck. In those situations where we were involved as a family, he would conform; we, in turn, would "get off his back" about what he wore in his private life.

For a lot of parents, including ourselves, shifting gears from control over a child into acceptance of an adolescent-nearly-adult making his or her own decisions and having a voice in what goes on in his or her life and the family's life isn't an easy transition. If the adolescent is still financially dependent, it's even harder. Nags and reminders are really voices of authority, and parents don't give up authority easily.

Once parents become aware of what they are doing and when they do it, they've come a long way towards changing. When we understood wanting our son to dress more conventionally was to please us and not him, we could strike a bargain that made life easier in some situations.

Learn to substitute some other behavior for nagging whenever you get the impulse to nag.

Parents can use a wide variety of substitutes when the impulse to nag occurs. One parent decided to say something complimentary to her adolescent son whenever she felt like nagging him. At first her substitute compliments seemed forced and artificial to both her son and herself, but they realized that she was sincerely trying to break a long-established habit, and they accepted this initial awkwardness. After a while, the substitute behavior became more and more natural, and the frequency of her nagging decreased dramatically.

A man we worked with decided to write a note to himself

whenever he felt the impulse to nag his adolescent daughters. In the beginning he found himself writing so many notes that he was astonished at how often he wanted to remind one of the daughters of some minor issue. After only two weeks, both he and his daughters reported that his nagging had disappeared almost entirely, and the father said that his need to even write notes to himself was becoming less and less frequent. There is no ideal substitute for everyone; each of us has to determine for ourself the kind of substitute behavior that will work. But once the substitute behavior has been decided, stick with it consistently regardless of how awkward it may at first seem to be.

Appreciate the side benefits of non-nagging.

Parents who go through this process of stopping their nagging almost always report certain positive consequences. First, there are side benefits in working with your adolescent on a joint problem. Although the nagging may have been the occasion of some terrible family battles in the past, the adolescent will appreciate the fact that the parent recognizes the problem and is trying to do something about it—by changing the parent's own behavior rather than blaming the adolescent. Moreover, doing this with the help of the adolescent reaffirms the parent's honest concern and humanity. Perhaps the most important and the most rewarding consequence is the decrease in family stress. When parents stop nagging, the number of arguments drops sharply, and both parents and their adolescents have a chance to learn how to live together without the irritation of petty bickering.

An interesting result we have noticed on a number of occasions is a change in the adolescent's behavior that had been the focus of nagging. The adolescent, for example, who has been nagged about not doing homework begins to do the work after the parents stop nagging about it. This

suggests that sometimes nagging actually provokes the un-
desired behavior. When parents are able to break the habit
of nagging their adolescents, they soon learn that tolerating
the minor irritants that once led to a parental nag is a small
price for the relationship one can have in a nagless family.

Guidelines for Rational Parenting

A very useful way to check on your own parenting behavior
is to keep a diary. Without this kind of systematic record
keeping most of us are likely to forget about what we have
done and thus obscure our own self-awareness. So, every
night for a week, before you go to sleep, write down the
answer to the following questions:

What suggestions, reminders, orders did I give my adolescent today? (For example, "Remember to do your homework." "Don't forget to take out the garbage." "Did you
brush your teeth?" "Get a haircut.") What were these
about? How many were there?

What did I criticize my adolescent about today? How
many times? How did I express my criticisms? How many
times did I praise my adolescent today? What exactly did I
praise? How did I express my praise?

After you have kept your parenting diary for a week, you
can put together the results and get an idea of your suggesting, reminding, ordering, criticizing, and praising behavior.
Just keeping the diary will probably influence what you do
for the week. Nevertheless, it's a good way of getting an
overall picture of how you behave in relation to your
adolescent.

Ask your adolescent to also keep a diary answering the
same questions you do. During that week don't talk about
what either of you has written. Then, after the week is up,
trade diaries and each of you read what the other has

written. How much do you agree and disagree? What were
the disagreements about?

Talk over the results with your adolescent. Together, identify the issues that bother you most, and then explain why
they bother you. But in the discussion, be sure to focus on
your feelings, the way *you* experienced what happened;
don't project the blame onto your adolescent. Above all,
don't fall into the role of prosecuting attorney. Don't try to
build a case to prove your adolescent guilty. Stick to your
feelings.

Then, listen to your adolescent's reactions. Try to get a
sense of how your adolescent has experienced what happened this past week. How does your adolescent feel about
your suggestions, reminders, orders, criticisms?

On the basis of your discussion, both of you should have a
clearer understanding of what triggers your critical reactions,
how you feel about these events, and how your adolescent
experiences what happens. Your next step is to work out
jointly some possible solutions. In all likelihood, you will
probably discover that both of you contribute to the difficulties that arise. On the one hand, your adolescent may do
things (or not do things) that are legitimate cause for concern; on the other hand, you may be especially sensitive to
certain issues or overly concerned about some problems and
as a result overreact to your adolescent's behavior. In any
event, think together about how both of you can modify
your behaviors, empathizing with each other's point of view,
and respecting each other's feelings. In working out your
solution together, aim at being realistic, concrete, and
down-to-earth. Don't expect miraculous changes overnight,
but work together on a day-to-day basis, incorporating the
basic principles of rational parenting into everyday life.

Think about the things your adolescent does that you feel

deserve praise. In the rush of everyday life you may have overlooked some of these praiseworthy behaviors, but if you take a few moments to think about them, you may discover that your adolescent does a lot more positive things than you have been aware of before. Without being artificial about it, without faking it or putting on an act, make sure your adolescent knows that you recognize and appreciate these aspects of his or her behavior.

Right to Privacy

*Remember that your adolescent has a right to
privacy, and regardless of your concerns,
you must respect that right.*

"How was the party last night?" we asked our son.
"Fine."
"Who was there?"
"People."
"Like who?"
"Kids."
"Seniors, juniors—who?"
"I didn't ask."
"How many?"
"Next time I'll take a census."
"Was there food?"
"Yeah."
"What kind?"
"Party food."
"Like what?"

"Cut it. Am I supposed to take notes? I went to a party. Is this a third degree examination?"

"What are you getting so angry for? All we are doing is asking a few questions. Is there anything wrong with our wanting to know where you were and what you did?"

"You're darn right. There's a lot wrong. Can't you understand there are some parts of my life I want to keep for myself? Do you have to know everything? Next time I go to the bathroom, I'll write a report."

There was a time when our children returned home from parties filled with stories of their experiences. We relished the descriptions. We were proud of their ability to fill in details so that we had a sense of having actually been on the scene with them. "The hotdogs were big. They had little baskets with candy-jelly beans. I had mostly red jelly beans. I traded some reds for greens."

We listened, asked probing questions, and smiled approvingly at the embellished replies. It is difficult for parents who have shared the lives of their children to accept the fact that during adolescence a strong need for privacy develops.

Thus, when a child is young and we ask the question "Where are you going?" the response might be "To Jimmy's house. We're going to play ball. Then I'm going to the store. My glue dried up. I want to finish the model. I need a quarter and a dime. I'm taking my bicycle. Goodbye."

"Don't be late for supper, dear."

The exchange undergoes a marked and sudden shift during adolescence. A reply to the same question "Where are you going?" might be answered with a mumbled "None of your business," or no answer at all.

"What are you going to do?"

"Stand on my head."

"Don't give me those kinds of answers."

"Then don't ask questions."

"Will you be home for supper?"

"That depends."

"Depends on what? Are you listening to me? I asked are you coming home for supper?"

"I was thinking about something. What did you say?"

For us and for many parents, the realization that our adolescents had private lives that were not shared with us was a difficult fact to accept. Curiosity as well as concern was part of our motivation in submitting them to what they called a "third degree" when we asked questions about where they had been or what they were doing. When a teenager returns home at three in the morning or on occasion fails to come home for an entire night, parents "climb the walls." A parent wants to know where the teenager has spent the night; a parent feels he or she *should* know, so when a teenager does eventually wander in the front door, the first reaction is to turn vindictively and ask, "Where the hell have you been?"

There is certainly nothing wrong with parents wanting to know where their adolescent has been, especially if the adolescent has stayed out later than usual. But the *way* parents communicate their concern is all important. The essential issue is concern about the adolescent, and parents can express this concern openly and honestly without being vindictive or threatening. The important point to remember is that adolescents have a right to privacy in their lives. If parents keep this thought in mind, they can convey their genuine concerns to their adolescents without also conveying the feeling that they are trying to intrude on what is legitimately private.

Learn to live with the fact that your adolescent has a private life that is not shared with you.

This remarkably simple solution to not invading an adolescent's privacy is without a doubt extremely difficult for interested parents. Not asking a straightforward question —for example, "Where have you been?"—the minute the adolescent appears in the house takes considerable self-control. But resisting that temptation has helped us as well as other parents. When our teenagers failed to show up near the dinner hour, we had dinner; and when they made a belated entrance, we merely stated that we had already eaten. Their dinners were put aside.

We feel confident that parents will discover as we did the less we asked the more was volunteered. We recall one night when we had gone into our bedroom, determined not to get up when we heard a wandering adolescent's footsteps in the front hall. Much later there was a knock at the door.

"Yes?"

"It's Jeff."

"Hi, Jeff."

"Can I come in?"

"Sure."

He sprawled across the foot of the bed and started asking us what we had done that night.

"Not much."

We managed to stop right there instead of continuing with a question about what he'd been doing. The silence was painful. Finally he got up and said, "I guess there's no use talking to you people. You don't seem very interested in what I've been doing." Another lesson learned. Accepting the fact that our teenager had a right to a private life was all well and good, but we had to avoid the opposite extreme. Teenagers must be allowed a private life, but as parents we have to make sure to watch for cues from them and share when they want to share.

We also found out that despite adolescents' egocentricity, they are curious about what their parents are doing. If we wanted our adolescents to share parts of their private lives, we discovered that we had to be willing to share aspects of our lives with them, too.

A normal aspect of teenage development is the need for privacy. The central psychological issue is the adolescent's growing sense of becoming an individual, separate and distinct from one's parents. The importance of this process of individuation in healthy psychological development cannot be overemphasized. It is a crucial part of the transition from childhood to adult; every adolescent who makes this transition successfully achieves a sense of being an individual, certainly in a continuing relationship with other members of the family but also an independent and unique person in his or her own right.

Show the same kind of respect for your adolescent's privacy that you would show for any adult in your family. For example, don't open your adolescent's mail unless your adolescent specifically requests you to do so; don't listen in on your adolescent's telephone conversations; don't insist on talking about a particular topic when you find your questions go unanswered and your adolescent tries to withdraw from a conversation. In general, stay out of affairs that are legitimately your adolescent's private concern.

Lack of privacy ranks high among adolescents' complaints about parents. After discovering her mother had been reading her diary, a teenage girl reported that she started keeping two personal records. One diary was left on her desk, and the other was hidden in a closet where she knew her mother would never find it. "I know my mom reads what I write because she'll ask me a question or say something which I know she could only find out from my diary."

From the parents' point of view their curiosity has good grounds. "I like to know what goes on in my son's life," said one mother. "It keeps me young in my attitudes."

Whatever the motivation, a remarkable number of parents have admitted to various forms of privacy invasions. The most obvious method is direct or indirect questioning.

"Where are you going? What will you do? What time will you be home? Who are you going with?"

"What's in the box in your closet? Old comic books? Are you reading comics at your age?"

"Why the long face? Did you have a fight with your boyfriend/girlfriend last night? I couldn't help hearing you on the porch. I wasn't listening. You were speaking loud enough to wake up the neighbors."

Another less desirable tactic some parents admitted using and feeling guilty about involved checking a youngster's room or possessions. "I couldn't stand it any longer. I was shocked at the magazines in his drawer. I asked him where he got hold of such things."

"The first knowledge I had of my son's interest in that phony religious group were some pamphlets in his wastebasket. I'm not sorry I found them. I would never have known about what he was thinking. It was an accident I found them; I asked him and he got angry. He said he wasn't interested in the group. Someone had just given them to him, and he tossed them out. He said I didn't have any business going through his wastebasket."

Some degree of privacy is a necessary condition for achieving a sense of individuality. Although we emphasize repeatedly the importance of communication between parents and adolescents, at the same time we must recognize that just as parents have a legitimate need for privacy, so too do their adolescents. As a matter of fact, this need is so important and so compelling that we can appropriately say that the adolescent has a *right to privacy.*

Make sure your adolescent has a chance to be alone when the adolescent feels the need to be alone.

In concrete terms this means some degree of physical privacy, a place where the adolescent can go off alone, though the specific way this is achieved depends upon the living arrangements within each family. There must be a corner, a physical space that can serve as the adolescent's territory. The space must be off limits to everyone else in the family.

One mother agreed about privacy but said that she found the litter in the room impossible. The daughter showed no concern for her possessions. The knowledge that one room in the house was a physical disaster upset her. "All I do is go in and straighten up. I find she keeps everything, even scraps of paper." Going in to put a room in order is a good way of finding out what is going on in a youngster's life. It's pretty hard not to take a quick look at what's written on scraps of paper when one is ostensibly cleaning.

We were no different from many parents. We did look at the notebooks in the middle of the floor. We did see things in the closet that weren't our affair. All this was disturbing until the day we imposed a simple rule on ourselves. The door of our boy's room was to stay shut no matter what occurred. Unless specifically invited, this was his physical space, his retreat, his place to do with as he pleased. With the door closed, a lot of pressure was off—both him and us.

The size of the space, of course, depends on the home. But even when the space is limited, a solution is possible. In one case a locked file cabinet in the corner of a living room made the difference between an angry teenage girl and her mother. The cabinet was the daughter's world "to fill with as she pleased." Notes, diaries, all were stored safely and securely.

Discoveries about the private life of an adolescent don't always occur through room searches. One parent admitted that the discoveries came when she was doing laundry. "I have to look in pockets of shirts and pants before I throw them into the wash." One hardly reaches into a pants pocket, we agree, with closed eyes, withdrawing some object and putting it aside without noticing it. However, the hidden secrets discovered more often than not are hardly worth the family battles that may result. It would have been far more helpful to both this youngster and his mother if she had insisted that the adolescent take care of his own laundry. "He'd never wash his own clothes," the mother told us. "I couldn't have him walking around with pants that had never been washed in a month." Unwashed clothes, however, would do more for the long term relationship than would the clean clothes and invasion of privacy.

For a teenager to have real privacy, parents must retreat from his or her physical presence. Getting out of sight even for short periods of time can help reduce the tension. And, just as an adolescent needs escape from a parent's physical presence, the parent needs the same kind of withdrawal. This is very clearly recognized with young children. The best therapy for a mother/father and a baby is that time when a sitter takes over. Parents soon learn this fact. What is sometimes forgotten is that the same kind of getting away is a must for adolescents and adults. Not everyone can take a vacation away from home to get out of sight. However, even though you live in the same house, reducing interaction can go a long way toward achieving the same goal.

Much-needed breaks can be worked into every family's routine. One family discovered that it can be as simple as not having dinner together every evening. The father, in this case, routinely had dinner time "angry words" with his daughter. No sooner had the family sat down together at the dinner table when the telephone would ring. One or another of the daughter's friends would call. Dinner time was sacred in the family. When she was told not to speak to

her friends while the family had dinner, she became sullen.
For the parents it was a simple request of no phone calls during the dinner hour. For the daughter the right to talk to her
friends when she pleased symbolized her independence.
The solution—separate dining hours—relieved the family
stress.

Families have their own rituals which they develop over
the years. Adolescents invariably challenge some of them.
What is remarkable when one steps back is how trivial some
of these rituals are and yet how they can assume major proportions. In fact, these rituals frequently spark the privacy
issue. Going over to relatives' homes for family gatherings
was a tradition in John's family. Shortly before the family
was going to get together again at one of their relative's
homes, John announced that he wasn't going with his family. He didn't give any reasons for his refusal; he just wasn't
going. This might have triggered a family argument if his
parents had insisted he come with them. But instead of
making John's refusal a serious matter, his parents made no
comment nor did they ask for reasons. They respected John's
right to privacy and the incident passed with no disagreement or hard feelings.

Even more important than physical privacy is psychological privacy: the right *not* to share, *not* to communicate, *not*
to talk—in short, the right to be alone.

"What's bothering you?"

"Nothing."

"I thought . . . "

"You thought wrong."

"Well, you seem very quiet."

"I like to be quiet. That doesn't mean anything's wrong.
I don't feel like talking."

Silence in our culture is regarded with suspicion. We

assume that something must be wrong if the adolescent isn't chattering, laughing, giggling, spewing out words. We expect some form of noise, whether it's the adolescent's own voice or noise from radios, hi-fi sets, or TV. So, when the teenager enters the house and doesn't "bubble" or react, parents immediately conclude that there's a problem brewing.

Parents sometimes find their adolescent's withdrawal hard to take because the adolescent at these times often seems lonely, perhaps melancholy, and even unhappy. Thus, the parent tries to relieve this apparent loneliness by making repeated efforts to find out what is bothering the teenager, to talk about it, to share the troubles—only to be met by the teenager's further withdrawal, leaving the parent confused and worried.

When your adolescent psychologically withdraws and seems lost to the rest of the world, remember that these periods of withdrawal may have tremendous significance in your adolescent's development. Don't mistake aloneness for loneliness. Be ready to listen, ready to offer support, but don't impose yourself. Above all, respect your adolescent's right to privacy.

When our adolescents retreat into their psychological shell, we must remember that aloneness is not the same thing as loneliness. All of us spend a great deal of our lives relating to one another, and certainly for the teenager, relationships with other teenagers as well as with some adults are tremendously important. Perhaps at no other time of life is peer group support more important and peer group influence more strongly felt than during adolescence.

Everyone, and especially the adolescent, needs time alone, physically and psychologically separated from other people. These are the moments when we can confront ourselves without having to relate to others, moments when we may experience ourselves most intensely and most directly, and in this experience discover who we are. For teenagers, whose chief psychological task is to establish and realize their own identity, these moments of self-confrontation and self-discovery are crucial and must be appreciated, valued, and respected by parents and other adults in their lives.

Frequently, periods of introspective withdrawal may have a melancholy air about them, but this form of adolescent melancholy must be distinguished from feelings of sadness or depression. The adolescent, after all, is facing some of the most profound questions of life: Who am I? Who will I become? What is the meaning of my life? What should I believe? What should I commit myself to? We don't mean that every adolescent is a solemn philosopher who spends a great deal of time pondering the universal issues of existence. This is certainly not the case. But every adolescent from time to time is concerned with the issue of personal commitment in one form or another, with beliefs, values, choices that have far-reaching consequences. For the teenager these are not abstract academic questions; they are immediate personal problems that relate directly to the central issue of establishing one's individuality and identity as an adult.

Moreover, the adolescent is consciously and actively moving away from childhood status and roles. This necessarily requires giving up some of the comfortable and rewarding aspects of childhood: the one-way dependency on parents, the freedom from any major responsibility, the protection usually accorded younger children.

"I'm not a kid any longer," one sixteen-year-old girl said. She felt her mother continued to treat her as a child. "She even tells me to take an umbrella if it's raining. She can't get it through her head that I'm not six anymore."

At the same time, the process of development entails taking on some of the more demanding aspects of adulthood:
becoming more independent and learning to accept an in-
terdependent relationship with parents, assuming greater
responsibility for one's choices and actions, and living
without the protective safeguards of childhood.

It should not be surprising or disturbing, therefore, to
sense a very serious, grave, weighty, perhaps even melancholy emotional tone when the adolescent becomes introspective and withdrawn. As parents it is sometimes difficult
for us to accept the fact that our adolescents must face some
of the most serious issues of their life without our immediate
and direct help. We may feel that with our experience, having learned from our own mistakes, we can save our children
from the trials and errors of growing up. We try to help by
offering advice, sharing the hard-earned wisdom that might
have benefitted us when we were their age. In our concern
we are apt to forget what we knew so well during our own
adolescence: There are times when every teenager must be
alone, must face the issues of growing up without the direct
aid and guidance of parents or any other adult. At these
times, parents can be most helpful by being ready to listen
when listening is called for, ready to offer support when support is asked for, but sincerely respecting the adolescent's
right to privacy.

Guidelines for Rational Parenting
Check the living arrangements of your family. Does your
adolescent have someplace where he or she can be alone and
entirely private? If not, how can this be arranged without
seriously inconveniencing others in the family?

What are the ways in which you or others intrude on your

adolescent's privacy? After you have thought about this yourself, talk with your adolescent about this issue and get his or her views of the matter. But in your conversation, don't be defensive when your adolescent tells you about how you are intrusive. Remember to listen without interrupting, without trying to explain your behavior or make excuses. Your aim is to understand your adolescent's point of view.

Are there some things about your adolescent's private life that bother you? In thinking about this question try to identify *why* they bother you. Then distinguish the legitimate rational concerns from the nonrational concerns. The rational concerns are those based on realistic factors that are likely to influence your adolescent's life. For example, the use of drugs or the development of dangerous driving habits could very well be realistic and rational sources of concern. Nonrational concerns are those that stem primarily from your own personal worries and probably don't have much to do with your adolescent's life. These might include, for example, your adolescent's manners, telephone usage, or styles of dress.

After you have identified these rational concerns in your own thinking, talk with your adolescent about them and explain the rational basis of your concerns. Express your feelings about them, but be sure to express these feelings so that they are clearly *your* feelings. Use *I-messages* that begin with "I feel"; avoid attacking or putting the blame on your adolescent; then listen to your adolescent's reactions to your concerns. Don't prejudge what your adolescent has to say; listen to understand.

How do you feel when your adolescent withdraws from you? Do you feel hurt, rejected, left out of your adolescent's life? When this happens, do you try to impose yourself on your adolescent? If you do, think of other ways to behave, other things you might do that will resolve your feelings and at the same time show respect for your adolescent's need for privacy.

Are there ways in which your adolescent intrudes on your own privacy? How do you react when this happens? Share these feelings with your adolescent, and then, together, work out some ways in which both of you will show mutual respect for each other's privacy.

Ups and Downs

Learn to live with your adolescent's ups and downs without overreacting, without trying to make too much sense of them, and without getting caught in the emotional roller coaster.

Our son, sixteen years old at the time, returned home from school. He walked up the driveway, kicked open a storm door. The key fumbled in the lock. Curses. The door opened, slammed shut, and a book bag was flung into a corner of the living room. Hiking boots scraped black tread marks on a polished wood floor. A refrigerator door opened, food pushed aside. A carton of milk spilled.

"Not a damn thing to eat." A jacket was tossed onto the kitchen table.

"What happened?"

"What makes you think anything happened?"

"Something bothering you?"

"Where did you get that idea? Just because I walk in the house without a smile you get at me—Is there something wrong?"

"You seem off," we answered.

Silence. He slouched out of the kitchen, sprawled on the floor in the living room hands behind his head staring up at the ceiling.

There are days in an adolescent's life that reach unbelievable lows. That morning he had left the house in a good mood. That evening he was sullen and unresponsive. In between, a maddening series of events had sent him plummeting downwards. He was late for a class and had to scrounge for an excuse, which wasn't accepted. After French he had gone out of his way to position himself at a staircase where a girl in whom he was interested usually passed on her way to algebra. She decided to go to her locker and didn't appear. In math class an examination was returned, and the results are better left undiscussed. That same girl who should have been at her locker at the end of the school day suddenly decided to have a long, intimate chat with a girl friend. And finally, before returning home he had decided to buy a piece of pizza. Instead of a freshly baked piece, he was handed a cold slice, which had obviously been prepared much earlier in the day. The crust tasted like soggy paste.

"Come on now," we told him after reviewing the day's disasters. "It's not the end of the world."

"In whose opinion?" he retorted.

And with that bit of wisdom we knew we were in for another session of teenage blues.

Living with an adolescent is sometimes like riding a roller coaster of emotional ups and downs. At one moment the adolescent may be riding high on a burst of optimism, self-confidence, and carefree joy, and then without warning plummet into the depths of depression, pessimism, and anxious self-concern. From an adult's point of view, neither the ups nor the downs make any sense, but regardless of whether or not they make sense, for the teenager these emotional reactions are undeniably real and psychologically meaningful. Therefore, a parent has to learn to live with these ups and downs, accept them as genuine, treat them with respect and understanding, and yet not get caught in the emotional roller coaster of the adolescent's life.

Neither extreme of the adolescent's up-and-down cycle may be easy for parents to take, though living through the ups is certainly less trying than dealing with the downs. When the adolescent's emotional life is on the upswing, there is likely to be more noise in the house—more music, more movement, more talking, more of everything that might jar the peace and tranquility of family life. Sometimes there may be a certain manic quality about the adolescent's activities with perhaps grandiose, expansive plans, and a sense of excitement that parents might find a little overwhelming.

Don't over-react to the occasional emotional lows your adolescent is bound to experience.

We were present one evening when the son of one of our friends presented a plan reflecting adolescent mania to his father, a reserved, middle-aged man who usually managed to maintain a calm perspective on most problems in daily life.

Rick, eighteen years of age and a college freshman, was a philosophy and language major. During high school he had edited the school's literary magazine and he wanted to become a writer, but that evening Rick enthusiastically announced that he and his friends planned to open a delicatessen service for students in the dormitory. He told his father that students study late, get hungry, and have no place to eat. The only thing the school missed was a late night delivery service of sandwiches and snacks. He and two friends, classmates in a philosophy seminar, were going to rent a refrigerator, buy food and take orders. The father listened to the outline of the project in a stupor.

"What the hell do you know about sandwiches—except to eat them?"

"I know a lot about them," Rick replied. Ignoring his father's sarcasm, Rick brought out the menu the boys had designed. One of the boys was an artist and had drawn pictures of various sandwiches. Rick and the other boy had written poetic descriptions of their offerings, assigning the sandwiches names—derived largely from Greek mythology. Among others, there was a Prometheus Special (ham and cheese on rye) and a Narcissus Delight (peanut butter and jelly on a sesame seed roll).

"This is what I pay tuition for?" asked the father.

Again Rick ignored the reaction and began to read the descriptions aloud, obviously relishing the twists of poetic phrase.

"What do you think it's going to cost you to start the business?" his father inquired.

"We got it figured out that we can make enough money this next term to go to Europe for the summer."

For the rest of the evening the father took apart the boy's plan step by step. While the son fantasized about how he would spend the profits, his father with pencil and paper in hand pointed out basic costs of operating a business. While the son described the intriguing menu he and his friends had devised, his father discussed the realities of obtaining loans, insurance costs, problems of partnerships and contracts. The son's dream was punctured by reality. The father had made his point. Neither spoke to each other by the end of the evening.

In the excitement and enthusiasm of the moment, the young man had been swept away by his imagination. But his father, with his eye firmly on "reality," had managed to thoroughly deflate his son's enthusiasm. Rather than burden his son with the hard facts of reality while the young man was enjoying a burst of unbridled optimism, the father would have done better simply to have accepted his son's high spirits and shared the enjoyment of the moment. Later on, when the mood shifted a bit, there would have been plenty of opportunity to face stubborn reality together without a needless battle.

When adolescents are on the upswing, they are likely to make all kinds of exciting plans that may have little to do with reality. Watch your timing; don't throw cold water on their enthusiasms. Learn to go with the flow, and later on when their enthusiasm for a particular plan has cooled a bit, there will be plenty of time for practicality.

Part of the motivation for parents injecting a note of reality into adolescents' fanciful plans comes from a protective desire. The father of the budding business student defended his behavior by saying that he couldn't stand by and see his son get in "over his head."

When children are small and are learning to ride bicycles, they often start off with training wheels. Parents feel the same way about activities later in life. One doesn't plunge; one gets experience, training wheels, before going off on some adventure. As we get older, we tend to lose some of the feeling that we can do *anything*, and we become cautious. The joy of adolescence comes from the enthusiasm and belief that *anything* is possible. And sometimes, perhaps more often than we might realize, this turns out to be the case.

We learned this important lesson through an incident in our own family. One son was always coming up with improbable plans, and with typical parental reality, we managed to put a damper on some of the schemes.

However, when it came to one particular decision, we failed completely. In late adolescence he announced that he was going to become a polo player. We were stunned. From our perspective, polo was impractical and absurd considering his limited experience with horses. As a little boy he had had a toy rocking horse. Several times during childhood he had been taken to zoos and put astride a pony. For fifty cents he had been led around a ring. On one occasion the pony broke out of a slow walk and our son, the future polo player, had insisted on getting off. Given this background with horses, he didn't seem much of a candidate for polo.

We could hardly enter into a discussion of his plans with much enthusiasm. For a while, we did our best to dissuade him, arguing that he didn't know how to ride, didn't have the vaguest idea of the sport, having seen polo played only once in his life. But we failed to convince him. He reacted angrily. Why couldn't we show more excitement and interest in his plans? None of the rational reasons for our lack of enthusiasm had any effect. During the next year he spent every spare moment either on a horse or falling off a horse. But he learned to ride. And our own attitude shifted when we realized that if he had decided to take up tennis, we would have been fired up with enthusiasm. We liked tennis. The fact that he had chosen an activity not of our own experience seemed to be the only reason for our reaction. Our behavior changed overnight. His next birthday gifts were boots and a helmet. The sport that interested him suddenly interested us. Within a year and a half, after repeated falls and a long stint on crutches, he made the school's polo team; and after the last game of the season, he came home with a trophy as a member of a winning team.

After his success we talked about our initial negative reactions. He wondered why, in the beginning at least, we had shown such skepticism. Why hadn't we been excited and enthusiastic? We told him that, at first, the whole notion of polo playing had struck us as outrageously impossible. He admitted that there were many times he had wanted to give up. What kept him going?

"I was going to prove to you and myself you were wrong."

Another underlying reason for parents witholding enthusiasm for some of the plans their adolescents propose stems from the fact that a parent's emotional reactions usually don't shift as rapidly or as strongly as do those of an adolescent. As a result, it may be hard for the parent to empathize with the adolescent's intense excitement.

As parents, we may feel we can't keep pace with adolescents who are one day going to open up sandwich delivery services, the next become actors or actresses, and on another day perhaps race track drivers. Not getting in the way, not putting up obstacles, and above all not coming up with the cold water of reality are undoubtedly the best things parents can do if they can't share the enthusiasm.

"My mother wasn't what you could say thrilled," Susan, a seventeen-year-old, told us, "when I told her I was going to buy an old car and learn how to get it running. But she never stopped me. She was pretty surprised when I got the car to work all by myself. I had a little help but not from anyone in the family."

Obviously, not every plan an adolescent makes is going to succeed. Some may not get beyond the excited dreaming stage. The enjoyment for the adolescent might come in the planning. One adolescent told us that he liked to think about doing a lot of different things even though he knew most of his ideas wouldn't turn out. During these positive swings in their emotional lives, adolescents don't need or even want their parents empathetic reactions. Sometimes all that's needed is acceptance.

A parent's life becomes much more difficult when the adolescent's emotional life swings to the other extreme,

towards depression, sullen anger, painful self-con-
sciousness, irritability, and despairing pessimism. These
are the times when teenagers feel that everything is falling in on them, the world is no damned good, they are
clumsy clods, and the future is hopeless. Every parent of
an adolescent has suffered through these emotional
blues, and while most parents know enough about
adolescence to expect blues from time to time, they remain among the most trying and frustrating aspects of
parenthood.

The parents' sense of frustration often begins with a
failure to understand the cause of the adolescent's emotional nosedive. Life may seem to be going smoothly for
the teenager, when, for some inexplicable reason, things
begin to fall apart at the seams. This trauma may be set
off by some minor disappointment, an apparently trivial
failure, an imagined or perhaps real slight that, to an
adult, appears insignificant. Sometimes there isn't even
a minor or trivial cause; the adolescent simply enters a
period of spontaneous and sullen depression for no apparent reason, leaving the parent totally befuddled, confused, and frustrated.

One mother told us she had thought she was very clever.
She had deluded herself into believing her daughter's low
points were associated with menstrual periods, but then had
learned "it doesn't always work like that." Her daughter
went from one extreme to another, menstruation or not.
"She'll be giggling, manic, cleaning up her room, singing at
the top of her voice, and that evening at dinner the long face
appears. The other evening all I did was put my coffee cup
down in the saucer. She practically screamed at me. 'Do you
have to make so much noise with the cup?' It couldn't have
been an hour before that she was in the living room dancing

to records—having a hilarious time—singing at the top of her voice.''

As with many other parents, this mother was bothered not only by her daughter's emotional lows, but also by her inability to understand the reasons for her daughter's reactions. Interrogating teenagers when they are emotionally down is usually an exercise in frustration. The answers are typically monosyllabic, uninformative grunts that rarely lead to understanding and leave parents even more frustrated than before. As a matter of fact, the principal error most parents make at this point is trying to push the teenager for an explanation. These efforts merely serve to make the teenager even more depressed and eventually lead to withdrawal or to an explosion on the part of parent or teenager.

When your teenager plunges into an emotional low, don't start probing for an explanation.

By and large, teenagers suffering the pangs of despair are not just holding back precious information that will clarify the entire situation for their parents. For the most part, adolescents aren't aware of what makes them plummet into periods of depression, and the precipitating events are often so trivial that the teenager may be embarrassed to mention them.

One teenager described this sense of triviality and the feeling that somehow the apparent cause didn't match the depth of her emotional reactions. That morning she had combed her hair in what she had thought was a highly flattering dramatic style. Feeling pretty good about the way she looked, she had gone into the kitchen to say goodbye to her mother who was sitting at the kitchen table having a second cup of coffee.

''My mom looked at me and asked me what I had done to my hair. It looked different. I don't know what happened to

me. I got this feeling of choking. I felt like crying." The girl
had said goodbye and gone to school feeling depressed and
unhappy. She didn't know whether her mother liked or disliked the way she had her hair. Later she didn't even want to
discuss it with her mother. "If I tell her, she'll say she didn't
say anything to me. She'll say all she said was my hair was
different and I am too sensitive." Because of this seemingly
trivial incident, she had been depressed all day, and later on,
when her mother asked what was wrong, the daughter
couldn't answer because the morning incident obviously
didn't deserve an all-day depression. Thus, her mother remained baffled and totally unaware of what had triggered
her daughter's blues.

*Don't always expect to understand why your adoles-
cent gets depressed or sullen or angry. Learn to live with
these emotional ups and downs without really understanding them. If you try too hard to understand each
time your adolescent's mood goes up and down, you'll
just be adding one more source of frustration to your
life.*

The adolescent's ups and downs are partially explained by
the physical changes that occur during this period of life.
There are times when hormonal imbalances may predispose
the teenager to extreme emotional reactions, but these
physiological factors certainly don't tell the entire story.
Probably more important than the physical changes are the
psychological sensitivities that are a normal part of this stage
of development. Because of the adolescent's lack of self-
confidence, minor slights, trivial failures, and petty problems may take on enormous personal meaning for the
teenager and thus evoke much stronger emotional reactions
than seem warranted.

Although parents may be aware of their adolescents'

special sensitivities, they should not expect to understand what is going on every time their son or daughter becomes depressed or sullen or angry. On most of these occasions the adolescents themselves don't understand why they're feeling the way they do, and a hovering parent anxiously prying for the facts will only make matters worse. Therefore, parents must have faith that the period of depression will pass, that the emotional pendulum will eventually swing towards a happier state, usually without the parent's active intervention. Ideally, if parents can manage the role, they should be available as sympathetic listeners who are willing to hear about their teenagers' trials and tribulations without prying, without trying to make it all fit into a neat, rational package, and without giving much advice. Most important at these times is conveying a sense of understanding how the adolescent is feeling without giving in to the normal parental urge to get more actively involved in solving whatever problems seem to be foremost at the moment.

Be a sympathetic but nonprying listener.

This passive stance isn't easy for most parents to take. When they see their adolescents obviously unhappy, parents all too often react empathetically, trying to get at the root of the problem in order to *do* something about it. But the most effective "doing" for a parent at this point simply involves being available as a sounding board—a parental sounding board that doesn't send out anxious reverberations that only serve to intensify the adolescent's already unhappy feelings.

In our family our tendency to overreact to moody low periods has, according to one son, driven him "batty." "Concern is fine," he told us, "but you people carry it to the extreme." He said that if he wasn't always smiling, if he returned home from school with less than a happy expression, he had the feeling we were ready to jump at him with a barrage of questions. "I can feel your blood pressure going up. It makes me feel worse."

As an example of our behavior he cited an incident that had occurred just a few days earlier. He had been sitting on the steps lacing up his boots. Something in his face, a hint of woebegone feelings, a lost expression, prompted our question, "What's wrong?"

"Nothing's wrong."

"You sure everything's all right?"

"Of course I'm sure."

"Then why the long face?"

Despite his insistence that everything was "fine," as we watched him leave the house, shoulders slouched, feet seeming to drag, we were convinced that a problem was on his mind. And then we started our speculations. Just before he left the house, he had been on the telephone for an hour. It must have been the telephone conversation that had sent his mood plummeting downwards.

And seeing him in a low mood made us react with knots in our stomachs. Empathy was getting the better of us. Like many parents, the hurts of our children are far worse than any personal setbacks or low periods we might experience in our own lives. As adults, somehow we manage to get through our own ups and downs. But watching your own child when he or she is glum and morose brings out protective, parenting reactions.

When children are young, soothing them is relatively easy. You take the child on your lap and with some hugs and kisses, and maybe a lollipop or some ice cream, the tears usually change to smiles. But it simply isn't reasonable to take a 155-pound adolescent onto one's lap and say, "Have a peanut butter sandwich and tell Mummy/Daddy what's on your mind."

All the while he was gone, we speculated about the possible causes of his low feelings. Without facts we let our imaginations go, and by the time he returned home, we had become increasingly worried. Our voices and our anxious greeting reflected the misery we thought he was suffering and which we shared.

"You've got to tell us," we demanded when he returned.

"Tell you what?"

"Don't play games. You know what we mean. You left here an hour ago with something on your mind. It's pretty bad. Okay, that's what parents are for, to help." We were unrelenting in our probing, and by the time we finished grilling him, the earlier problem became a major issue. His story finally came out. He had been on the telephone with a girl friend. Things hadn't gone well (in the back and forth typical of these kinds of relationships). He had decided to take a walk and met some friends. They had stopped to play basketball, and he had returned home in a good mood. But when he met our barrage of "sympathetic" questions, his earlier despondency returned, and he felt worse than ever. Our probing had managed to make him feel really miserable and angry, and he shuffled off to his room, grumbling, "I don't feel like eating dinner; go ahead without me. I'll eat later."

We recall asking ourselves at the time, "What's gotten into him?" After all, we had just tried to show empathetic understanding and sympathetic concern. In our effort to be "good," understanding parents, we had managed to throw him back into the doldrums.

Life started going much more smoothly when we practiced what we have termed *attentive inattentiveness*. Given the stresses adolescents face today, there are bound to be lows. A concerned parent can't avoid seeing an adolescent's behavior or expression and being bothered by the "down" periods. However, we learned to guard against jumping in with a ready solution or a long talk, both of which at times magnified the problems of the moment. The next time we were told "I'll eat later," our response was "Fine, we'll leave your dinner."

When your adolescent is feeling low, go easy on the advice. Listening is much more valuable than telling at these times. And above all, don't get too actively involved in trying to solve whatever seems to be the adolescent's problem at the moment. Let your adolescent do most of the problem solving. Chances are the problem will disappear anyway when your adolescent's mood swings up again. At times, not asking what's wrong is much wiser than bombarding the adolescent with inquiries. A cooling-off period is all that may be needed.

In discussing their emotional ups and downs with us, adolescents have again and again repeated a common theme —their need for privacy, especially when they are feeling low. This point was made very clearly and dramatically by a sixteen-year-old girl who described her feelings when she was depressed.

At these low times in her life she didn't want to talk to anyone, least of all her mother or father. "I'd rather be by myself, in my room. I don't want either of them keeping at me." She especially reacted to a brother and sister who were younger. They were worse than her parents, bothering her, asking her to do things with them, or wanting to borrow some possession. Rather than relate to the outside world she wanted only to "crawl inside myself." She preferred not having anyone see her cry, and that's what she might do when she was down on the world and herself.

Respect your teenager's need for privacy—especially when your teenager is feeling low.

Throughout this discussion of adolescents' emotional ups and downs we have been referring to normal variations that occur in every teenager's life. Of course, if a teenager becomes seriously depressed and remains in that state for a relatively long period of time—perhaps for weeks or months —the problem may be something more than the normal variability of adolescent life, and it would be wise to seek professional advice. But for the vast majority of adolescents who go through cycles of emotional ups and downs, parents should remember that the most frequent parental errors stem from trying to do too much rather than too little. A little listening, some faith in the adolescent's ability to handle his or her own problems, and a lot of respect for the adolescent's right to privacy can go a long way towards making life easier for both parent and teenager during these times of stress.

There is another kind of "up and down" phenomenon that often baffles parents. Life for their adolescent may be going along smoothly, with clearcut signs of increasing maturity, growing self-confidence, and greater emotional stability. These are the times when parents get a sense of satisfaction from parenthood and may begin to feel that the storms of adolescence are finally over. Then, without warning, the whole process of growing up suddenly seems to shift into reverse. The gains in maturity seem to be lost. Self-confidence flies out the window; there may be temper tantrums, emotional instability, confusion; and the adolescent appears to be behaving more like a child than ever before.

After dinner one evening we asked our seventeen-year-old son to take out the garbage. The simple request evoked an unusually hostile reaction.

"You can't go one day without nagging me."

"What do you mean, nagging you? All we asked was that you take out the garbage. Is that too much to ask you to do?"

"What are you trying to tell me? That I don't do anything? Okay, I'm not good at anything."

"We didn't say that. All we said was to take out the garbage."

"If I'm that bad, I think it's about time I lived somewhere else," And with that comment he stormed out of the house.

Seconds later a rock crashed through the front storm door, grazing the paint off a side wall, and sliding across the kitchen floor. We looked at the rock in stunned silence. Our highly intelligent, mature, sociable, verbal, charming son of whom we were extremely proud had taken a rock and thrown it at the house. If we had ever been asked "Would your seventeen-year-old son haul off and throw a rock at his own house?" our immediate response would have been "Absurd. Never!" And here we were with shattered glass, scraped paint, and a gash on the floor tile.

Our instinctive reaction was to go out of the house, haul him back physically, and sit him down for a good lecture. How dare he behave like a four-year-old? We cleaned up the splinters, astonished how far the fragments had traveled. The work involved in cleaning up took the edge off our anger. Rationally, we realized that the way we behaved at this moment would affect our relationship.

He was standing in the driveway when we went out on the porch and asked him to come and sit down with us.

"You're pretty angry with me?" he asked.

"No."

"I'll clean up."

"It's all cleaned up. We can get a new glass tomorrow."

What was more important than glass, we told him, was how he felt. It was hard for us to believe that being asked to take out the garbage was enough to make him throw a rock. If he wanted to talk to us, we wanted to listen. If he didn't feel like talking, we'd just like him to sit with us.

Bit by bit he shared some of the frustrations of the past several days. Nothing, he realized, was earthshaking, but the growing tension was getting too much for him. There had been a French test that had gone awry when he expected a perfect grade. (He had forgotten to put in the accent marks.) A run-in with some friends over a game, a lost textbook, and several other trivial events seemed to pile up at once; and when we had asked him to take out the garbage, not once but several times, he felt that everything was tumbling down on top of him. He was powerless and worthless. He described feeling a kind of pressure inside, and he said he felt strangely relaxed after he threw the rock. "I haven't done anything like that since I was about four," he added reflectively. He remembered that time. He and several friends were playing in the park. One friend took our son's sandpail and shovel and refused to give it back. "I remember taking a rock and throwing it at him. I missed. He took the shovel and hit me in the forehead. I had to have stitches, didn't I?" Now he was feeling as if he had been reliving the earlier rock-throwing incident. (But this time, fortunately, no stitches were required.)

He told us he was sorry about the rock. According to him we had a right to yell, we had a right to punish him or make him feel worse than he did, but, he added, he was glad we hadn't "rubbed it in."

Don't expect progress toward greater maturity to be a smooth, ever-forward process. Expect regressions from

*time to time, periods in which growth seems to go
backwards and the adolescent acts more like a child
than an adult.*

These periods of temporary regression in which the process of growing up appears to go in reverse are absolutely normal and nothing to become overly concerned about. All of
us have gone through exactly the same pattern of
psychological growth and regression, even though we are
usually not aware of it. Psychological growth rarely proceeds
without brief periods of temporary regression, and during
adolescence, when the individual is rapidly moving towards
maturity, these regressions-in-the-process-of-growth are to
be expected. Thus, ups and downs in levels of maturity are a
normal part of teenagers' lives, and a teenager who acts like
an adult one day and a child the next is following a pattern
of behavior characteristic of all adolescents.

Parents sometimes react to these periods of regression as if
they were a major problem, and indeed, if too much attention is paid to them, they can become a serious problem.

*When your adolescent does regress, remember that
that is precisely the time to relieve external pressure.
Don't worry about these periods of regression; they are
part of the normal process of psychological growth.
They are most likely to be temporary, and given a
chance to relieve some of the tension that naturally
builds up in the course of growing up, the adolescent
will reintegrate and continue to mature.*

Cynthia's parents avoided a potentially serious problem
with their daughter through attentive inattentiveness. During her junior year Cynthia, who up until that time had
been a good student, stopped working. She went to her
room ostensibly to study as usual; however, when she
brought home her first report card, her grades showed that

she hadn't been doing any schoolwork during those hours. Instead of insisting that she work harder, get off the telephone every evening, stop watching TV on school nights, warning her of the dire consequences poor grades meant in terms of college applications, her parents let Cynthia take the lead in analyzing what was happening. When she admitted disappointment, they agreed. The grades were disappointing.

"You don't like my grades, do you?" Cynthia asked her parents.

"How do *you* feel about them?"

"I'm asking you; don't twist what I say around."

"They're your grades. It's important what you feel about them."

"They're lousy grades," Cynthia admitted. "I've never had such terrible grades."

"Don't say we didn't warn you. We've told you about watching TV on school nights, talking on the telephone. Nothing was important that couldn't have waited until after your work was done. How many times have we reminded you?"

"I don't need you to tell me. I don't need your lectures. Please don't keep telling me over and over again what I already know. Can't you understand I'm not a little girl anymore?"

At seventeen Cynthia had to come to her own conclusions about what was happening. Cynthia's parents started out being understanding and reflective, but their good intentions didn't last very long and they soon switched to lecturing Cynthia about all she had done wrong. Telling her what she already knew wasn't going to help her get out of the mood. She had to realize that she was hurting herself. At this point, it was far better to help Cynthia clarify and understand her own feelings and behavior, rather than blame her or give her a lecture about why she should work harder. She already knew she should work harder, and her parents could be most helpful by encouraging Cynthia to think about herself and try to gain some greater understanding of her experiences.

Don't make things worse by communicating your own anxiety to your adolescent.

If parents become worried because a teenager suddenly seems to be behaving childishly or performing poorly, their concern over the behavior may very well create tension, and the tension itself is likely to make the situation more difficult for the teenager. Growing up involves enough tension without having the added tension of unrealistic parental concern. Therefore, when a teenager goes through these periods of childishness, of immaturity and regression, parents must learn to pay as little attention to them as possible. If a parent finds it hard *not* to react, it may help to remember that in almost all instances, the less attention a parent pays to a bit of adolescent immaturity, the sooner that immaturity is likely to disappear.

Remember that in dealing with your adolescent's ups and downs, it is generally better to do too little than too much.

Guidelines for Rational Parenting

The best way to prepare yourself to respond to your adolescent's emotional ups and downs is to consider your own emotional experiences and think about the kinds of responses from others that were most helpful to you.

When you've been emotionally high, happily excited, maybe even a little manic, how would you have reacted to someone who insisted that you should come down to earth, be hardheaded, practical, use your "common sense"? Isn't it likely that that kind of reaction from someone else would turn you off, probably even irritate you?

And when you've been emotionally down, really depressed, how would you have responded to someone who kept probing for an explanation, demanded that you keep on talking, and pushed you to make sense of your feelings. When we are feeling low, most of us want a sympathetic ear available, someone who will listen if we want to talk, but who will also respect our need *not* to talk, our need to withdraw into our own psychological privacy.

It's certainly not easy for a parent to stand by while their adolescents are feeling low and depressed. And yet, it is precisely during these times that adolescents need someone who will stand by without intruding, who will be sympathetic without overreacting, who will be supportive without overburdening them with advice.

The Importance of Being Human

Be realistic about yourself; don't play the role of an all-knowing, all-powerful, always-right parent.

Many years ago we were sitting at the dinner table when one of our children, who was at that time six years old, announced, "Tommy's father is coming over."

"Why?" we asked. Tommy's father wasn't someone we knew well. In fact, our only relationship with Tommy's father had been several angry telephone calls concerning children's squabbles.

Our son played with some cookie crumbs, avoiding an answer. "Why?" we insisted. Why should Tommy's father pay us a visit?

A reluctant response was finally pulled from our son. "He's coming over to fight with Daddy."

"You must be kidding." Stunned, we probed further.

That afternoon our son and Tommy had had one of their frequent quarrels. Although we lost track of the course of their battle, it was very clear that Tommy and our son had volunteered their fathers as substitute opponents.

"My daddy can beat the hell out of yours."

"You want to bet? My daddy is a lot stronger."

Evidently each boy had recounted the physical prowess of their respective fathers, and a challenge match had been set up for that evening.

"Can't you beat him, Daddy?" our son asked.

"That's not the point."

"What's the point? You're strong enough, Daddy. You can beat him. Tommy's always bragging about his father. I told him my daddy is stronger."

"Did you ever see me fight?"

"No."

"Then you shouldn't talk like that."

"But you can, can't you?"

That evening, contrary to our usual habits, we went to an early midweek movie. No fight developed. The image of a strong, powerful father who could get the best of Tommy's father was preserved and luckily never put to the test.

At six it was important for our son to see his father as a strong, powerful figure, as someone who could effortlessly take care of another father. Not only did our son see his father as strong, but he had answers to questions, knew all about the world—in short, he was wise, knowledgeable, strong, and confident (particularly when certain challenges like the fight with Tommy's father could be cleverly avoided).

An important part of every adolescent's growing up is the discovery that parents are not really perfect. They are not the all-knowing, all-powerful, always-right people they might have seemed to be earlier in the child's life. The adolescent learns that, in fact, parents have their own hang-ups; that there are an awful lot of things parents don't know; and that they are far from always being right.

Although one might assume that this discovery is little more than recognizing the obvious and the mundane, the adolescent's response is often ambivalent. It is not easy to shake loose from old childhood beliefs about the perfection of one's parents, and in a way, thinking that Mom and Dad are strong, superhuman, protective figures can be comforting. But in the process of breaking away emotionally from earlier childhood dependency, an adolescent can be reassured by the realization that parents, once thought of in superhuman terms, are really just people like everyone else.

Take your child's idealization of you with a grain of salt; enjoy it while you can, but don't be surprised when the comments abruptly take on a more critical tone.

The daughter of a distinguished psychiatrist on the staff of a major medical center talked about her reactions to her first awareness that her father wasn't the center of the academic world. While she was growing up, she had looked up to him, feeling he was the most important person in the world. She had been awed by the attentiveness and respect his students showed him. During her first term in college she took a psychology course and felt very special when her father's name was listed among the many references. Friends also noted the name; however, one commented, "He's hardly Freud."

She felt hurt, depressed, and on her first visit home remembered blurting out the question, "Dad, how do you feel about not being Freud?"

The query came, the father reported, just at the time he was feeling rather good about some of his work. His first reaction was irritation and a sense of being hurt by his daughter's deflating remark. Instead of reacting defensively, however, he asked her how she felt about her discovery. Her comment was, "Sorry and glad, I suppose."

In one way she was disappointed to discover that while he was special to her, he was not super-special in the outside world. In another way she felt relief and guilt about being relieved. "I knew I had a chance; the other way, if Dad had been someone like Freud, I guess I would have felt hopeless.

Nothing I could do could match him."

This young woman's father clearly handled the situation with sensitivity and understanding. Rather than respond on the basis of his initial emotional reaction, he focused attention on his daughter's feelings; as a result, she was able to clarify her feelings about her father and about herself, and she took a major step towards resolving one of the important myths of her childhood. Instead of becoming an issue of threat and defense, this instance became a significant part of her growing from adolescence to adulthood.

Given the usual concerns, fears, and lack of confidence that characterize the adolescent period of development, there is a good deal of psychological security in having parents who are powerful enough to protect you from any threat. As a result, adolescents may tend to continue the childhood myth of parental perfection, despite plenty of evidence to the contrary. At the same time, adolescents resent this mythological omnipotence, because it threatens their own need for increasing independence.

Above all, keep your eyes on reality, especially about yourself, and be careful not to fall into the trap of mythological perfection. If you make a mistake, admit it, not with undue humility but with honesty. Few experiences are more reassuring to an adolescent than hearing a parent admit an error. Recognize and appreciate your own imperfections, and remember that it is far more important to be human and humane than to be always right.

If a parent appears to be overwhelmingly powerful, successful, and always "right," the adolescent may very well develop a sense of hopelessness in ever being able to achieve an acceptable adult status. Moreover, adolescents are often painfully aware of their own inadequacies, and their fears about themselves are easily magnified in relation to the mythical perfect parent. Parents can sometimes be too much of a good thing, and we often see adolescents trying to cut their parents down to size, criticizing them, attacking them, pointing out their weaknesses, faults, and defects in order to establish and reinforce the fact that they are humanly imperfect. In this way, adolescents both unrealistically idealize and unrealistically denigrate their parents, often swinging from one extreme to the other with barely a pause for breath.

Parents may sometimes bask in their children's occasional idealizations. After all, in a world that is not always appreciative of one's sterling qualities, it is undeniably pleasant to be viewed through the rose-tinted lens of an adolescent's idealization. However, that view can change abruptly, and it is just as undeniably unpleasant and threatening to be seen as old-fashioned, narrow-minded, ignorant, insensitive, and generally incompetent.

Parents sometimes react to their adolescent's criticism by striving to become even more powerful, more knowledgeable, more consistently right than ever before, and they are especially touchy when their adolescent children fail to recognize or appreciate their parental perfection.

For parents who might otherwise feel relatively immune to the barbs and insults of the outside world, it comes as a cruel blow when our own children cut us down to size. One mother told of the devastation she felt one afternoon when she had dressed up to visit her son's school. She had thought she looked extremely attractive, but her adolescent son's only comment when he saw her was "You're not coming to my school like that!"

"What's wrong?"

"Nothing."

"It's obvious that something's the matter."

"A lot of the parents will be coming."

"Well, so am I."

"Maybe you could dress up more, like you and Dad were going out."

"I don't understand what you're talking about. This is an afternoon at your school. No one dresses up."

"They don't wear pants—the mothers . . . "

"That's ridiculous. Everybody wears pants suits nowadays."

"Yeah?" asked her son quizzically. "With twenty pounds less," he blurted out.

Up until that point her son had never mentioned her weight. He hadn't been interested in what she wore, nor her appearance in general. The day of parents' visitation at school he became painfully conscious of his mother, the way she looked, the way she would appear in front of his friends.

One mother's comment about this incident was that she would have thrown that child out of the house for making that kind of remark, but we can say with confidence that no parent has escaped a taunt or two from an adolescent upon whom they may feel they have lavished attention, money, and love.

• "What have you ever done that's so great?"

• "You're not so hot. There are plenty of men—my friends' fathers—who make twice what you do."

• "You haven't got all the answers."

• "Look, ma, you're old-fashioned—you gotta face it. Times are different."

We could list numerous comments parents have heard that have made them feel wilted and bitter, and there's no question that the remarks hurt. There's no doubt that being told off by this kid in your house is a cruel low blow. As parents we like to think we deserve more than a hostile comment. We forget that when we were growing up we probably said some of the same things to our own parents.

One father told us that if his son or daughter ever talked back he wouldn't be above using force to bring the youngster back to his or her senses. It's very natural to want to lash back when an adolescent behaves in this way.

- "No child of mine will talk to me like that and get away with it."
- "How dare she say such a thing to me!"
- "If my son ever says anything like that again, he's had it as far as I'm concerned."

Just as you take your adolescent's positive comments with a grain of salt, also temper your reactions to the negative comments. Don't get caught in a defensive stance of trying to protect your ego from the potshots your adolescent will take from time to time. Don't confuse these potshots with a lack of love or respect; by and large, they reflect the normal growing pains of a healthy teenager who needs a human-sized parent.

Parents who lash back at their adolescents don't accomplish much by it. Shouting matches and exchanges of ridicule won't help matters. A verbal tug-of-war can only hurt and drain both the adult and the adolescent of energy. Admittedly, it's very tempting. There are times when we feel pushed to the limit. We can certainly be hurt by what our children say to us, and resisting the urge to tell off our child takes a lot of strength at these moments. But it helps to remember that when these kinds of situations arise, there is more than a touch of unreality in the perceptions of both parents and their children. Conflicts inevitably develop out of this unreality; the adolescents step up their attacks, become increasingly obnoxious and threatening, while parents become more rigidly insistent on being right, respected, and perfect.

There can be no satisfactory solution as long as the perceptions of parent or adolescent are distorted. Someone has to stay in touch with reality, and at this point parents are probably better suited for the responsibility.

Guidelines for Rational Parenting

As a result of the normal range of insecurities adolescents experience in the course of their development, adolescents are likely to be especially sensitive to any sign of adult "superiority." This is particularly true if the adult happens to be the adolescent's parent. Problems do not stem from the parent's position of authority in relation to an adolescent; given the responsibilities parents must assume and the relative inexperience of adolescents, this authority is simply a fact of life. However, for effective parenting, the relationship between parent and adolescent must be characterized by *rational* authority, and this is most likely to be achieved if the parent is aware of how he or she relates to the adolescent.

To gain this self-awareness think about your recent behavior in relation to your adolescent. When you haven't known something or have been unsure of yourself, have you felt free to admit your lack of knowledge or unsureness? Do you find yourself going out of your way to cover up your human imperfections, your shortcomings, your errors? When you have been wrong about something and an apology is appropriately in order, do you feel comfortable and confident enough to offer that apology to your adolescent? Or do you always expect the apologies from your adolescent?

The next time you are wrong about something in relation to your adolescent, regardless of whether it involves a trivial matter or an issue of greater importance, make sure that you explicitly admit to your adolescent that you were wrong, and if appropriate, apologize. And in your apology, provide a model for graceful, non-threatened admission of error. Obviously, we are not suggesting that you consciously make an error just so you can apologize and prove you are human. That, of course, would be absurd. But in the normal course of daily life, all of us from time to time are bound to make mistakes. No one is perfect. Therefore, the next time you are wrong, admit it. You don't have to make an issue of it. Just admit you were wrong, without a fuss or an excuse.

Think about the criticisms your adolescent makes of you. Are these criticisms a way of cutting you down to human size? How do you react? Are there some things about which you are especially sensitive? When your adolescent attacks these sensitive areas, do you become defensive and launch a counterattack?

The next time your adolescent says or does something that is hurtful to you, respond by saying that you are hurt—but don't become defensive or attack back. Simply report your feelings as you experience them. For your adolescent, discovering that a parent really feels hurt when attacked is an important part of recognizing the parent's humanity. But adolescents can make this discovery only when they don't feel threatened.

Overparenting

Don't overparent; give adolescents a chance to learn and grow up by making their own choices, their own decisions, and sometimes their own mistakes.

Adolescence requires a major shift in the role of a parent. During a child's infancy and later childhood, parents are expected to make most of the important decisions in their child's life. After all, the child's lack of experience and knowledge makes it necessary for parents to assume primary responsibility for the more significant choices affecting the child, and for the most part, children usually accept this state of affairs without a great deal of resistance.

Certainly there are times when the child will fight back and shout, "I won't go to bed," or "I'm not going to pick up my toys," or "I won't wear my boots." But most parents of pre-adolescent children can get their way. Until their children are adolescents, parents have several things going for them. They are bigger, stronger, can shout louder, and, if necessary, they can use force. An eleven-year-old who decides to stay at a party past midnight won't get very far if the parent disapproves. All the parent has to do is to go over to the house where the party is being held and insist the child come home. There might be objections, but nine times out of ten the parent will win that contest. However, a parent doesn't go over to a teenage party, ring the bell, walk in the house and tell a sixteen-year-old that "Mommy thinks it's about time you were in bed."

*When your child enters adolescence, be prepared to
shift your role as a parent. Don't try to hang on to old
patterns of parenting, even though this may mean
breaking habits that have been established over many
years.*

Striving for independence is a major psychological motivation of adolescence, and independence means gaining an
opportunity to make choices and decisions, not only about
minor matters of everyday life but also about issues that may
have long-term consequences. This developmental thrust for
independence is clearly a desirable, even necessary, part of
the adolescent's progress towards maturity. In our society, a
normal, psychologically healthy adult must be capable of
making independent decisions, taking into account the feelings and needs of other people, to be sure, but nevertheless
able to make choices on his or her own. This is an essential
aspect of being a mature person.

*As early as possible in your child's adolescence make
sure that there are plenty of opportunities for your
teenager to make truly independent choices and decisions.*

The capacity to make independent decisions doesn't appear overnight. One cannot shift from being a dependent
child to a reasonably independent adult without a good deal
of practice and experience in decision making. Therefore,
from a developmental point of view, the opportunity to
become increasingly independent, to make more and more
of one's own choices in both trivial and important matters is
crucial during adolescence.

But not all parents are prepared to accept this major shift
in responsibility. It's a whole changeover in parental role. For
too many years we've been playing the role of props, holding
up the toddler struggling to walk, giving support to a

youngster learning how to swim, running alongside two-wheeled bicycles offering steady hands when the bicycle starts to swerve and threatens to topple over. We've selected clothing; we've decided what to serve at mealtimes. For a lot of youngsters, the only choices they get a chance to make are insignificant, limited to selecting birthday or holiday presents, hardly enough practice for making decisions that can have profound effects on one's life. For parents, switching roles from decision makers to advisors isn't easy. As one father told us, "It's like being demoted in your job." After a dozen years of making the important decisions in a child's life, it isn't easy to give over this responsibility as rapidly as the child's psychological development warrants. Moreover, many parents become especially sensitive to the potentially negative consequences of a decision an adolescent might make.

One father was extremely upset by his adolescent's decision to take a year off between high school and college. The boy wanted to have an adventure, travel to another part of the country, spend time wandering. He had saved summer earnings, bought a car, and was determined to take off. The father was concerned about the rashness of his son's decision. He resented having to worry about this "crazy plan" because, as he put it, "I have my own worries." He had recently sold his business, taken out a large loan and was gambling on a whole new line of work. He felt pretty sure that things were going to work out, but at that moment it was "touch and go." To him, his son's fling had no real value; it was a waste of time. The father had a whole list of rational (and some irrational) points about why his son's plans were foolhardy. "The car is old; he will get out of the rhythm of going to school; he won't be doing anything worthwhile; education is most important at this age; going back to school after he is out for a year would be hard.''

As this example shows, parents may be quite willing to take chances in their own lives but be extremely cautious and conservative with respect to their teenagers. They see all kinds of possible dangers and difficulties, many of which may be real, and they become frightened that their relatively inexperienced, perhaps even naive, adolescent will make the ''wrong'' choices. They may even tend to magnify these dangers and underestimate the strength and resilience of their teenagers.

It is intriguing how adults forget events of their own adolescence. We were visiting old friends. At the time, they were in despair, frantically concerned about their nineteen-year-old son, who was rashly considering marrying a nineteen-year-old girl friend. They didn't want to live together; they wanted to be conventionally married. Both were college freshmen. The distraught parents had a whole list of arguments against the marriage. Getting married at nineteen was inviting future disasters. How would the couple manage to live? Why were they obstinately going ahead, plunging into a relationship so young? They should wait; they had no idea about the seriousness of the step. Misfortune after misfortune with regard to the future were outlined. The young man interrupted the gloomy lecture.

''How old were you when you got married?'' he asked them.

''Nineteen,'' they were forced to admit before quickly adding, ''It was different then, a lot different.''

There is nothing more irritating, and justifiably so, than parents criticizing their adolescents' plans and decisions, admitting to similar situations in their own youth, and then weaseling out of the argument by saying, ''It was different for us.'' The ''do as I say but not as I do'' code for behavior isn't one an adolescent is eager to accept.

Motivated by sincere concern, parents may become overly protective and overly cautious just when their adolescents need to try their own wings in the process of becoming adults. Thus, parents face a dilemma. On the one hand, there is a clearcut, compelling need for adolescents to practice independence in order to mature. Without this experience in being independent and responsible for one's own choices, the adolescent's development is seriously hampered. On the other hand, there are complicated problems that adolescents encounter, problems which they may not be adequately prepared to deal with. They may not have the knowledge or experience necessary to make the wisest choice in every instance, and their teenage decisions may have unfortunate long-term consequences.

For the conscientious parent there is no easy solution. However, as a start in resolving this issue, we suggest that parents focus on the *process* of decision making in their families. In this process, the parent's optimum role depends upon the nature of the decision to be made. For many of the choices adolescents make, parents should take virtually no responsibility.

In talking with adolescents, among the biggest hangups many voiced was parental interference about how money was spent. "I babysit," reported one seventeen-year-old. "It's my money. I'll go to the mall and buy something, and my mom'll have a fit. She says I have more clothes than I can wear, that I should save my money. I don't want to save my money. What's the money for if I can't get what I want?"

This adolescent's mother was in a constant battle over what she considered the spendthrift habits of her daughter. "She buys and buys constantly. She hadn't saved a penny of her earnings from the summer. There's a closet filled with junk records, she buys records, listens to them once, and most of them land up in the bottom of the closet collecting dust. It's wasteful. In this day and age it's criminal what she does.''

All of us parents suddenly acquire self-righteous streaks, playing the game as if we have spent a lifetime of being cautious, practical, and frugal. Obviously we aren't condoning wastefulness; but allowances, pocket money, an adolescent's own earnings should belong to the adolescent; and the adolescent should decide how to spend that money.

In dealing with issues such as money, clothes, hairstyles, to cite only a few examples which seem to ignite sparks in family relationships, we don't think the parent need take a totally passive role. The parent should make clear what the realistic limits are. For example, if money is involved, parents should be absolutely explicit about exactly how much financial support their teenager can count on. But once these realistic limits are spelled out, parents should remain interested observers, expressing opinions but not out to drive the teenager into misery about the errors in good judgment he or she may have committed—errors, we must keep in mind, from the parent's perspective.

In a discussion with a group of teenagers about behaviors they least liked in their parents, many commented, ''Making me feel guilty about how I spend money, the way I look, how I dress, manners.''

When children are small we can get away with saying ''If I were you, honey, I wouldn't walk around with my shoelaces untied. You can trip and fall and hurt yourself. Can you tie your shoelaces? Do you want Mommy or Daddy to help you?'' By the time a child reaches adolescence, the polite phrases disappear and we are more apt to say, ''Can't you change your sneakers? Is there any need to go around without shoelaces? What are you, some kind of bum?'' And if the footwear really is disturbing, the comments might even be stronger. ''It's sickening the way you dress. You have good clothes in the closet. I don't understand why you dress like you do.'' For the most part, parents have to learn to accept many of the choices and decisions their adolescents make without trying to make their teengers feel guilty about their behaviors.

Our advice, one parent told us, was all fine and good but what about the teenager who repeatedly makes the same mistake, won't seem to acquire the behaviors the parent is so eager to introduce. Ideally it would be great if an adolescent, or any person for that matter, would learn a lesson after some sensible instruction. With rare exceptions this doesn't happen. We need lots of trials and errors before we acquire new skills, new behaviors. When kids won't take good sound advice, it doesn't achieve any purpose to step up the pressure by guilt-inducing remarks.

Recognize and appreciate your adolescent's need to become increasingly independent and the need to practice this independence with the family before assuming the full responsibility of adulthood.

Permitting youngsters to make their own decisions early in adolescence is crucial. We may begin by allowing them to choose clothes and to spend pocket money as they wish, but clearly we have to extend the range beyond these simple matters. The more practice adolescents have with independent decision making, the better it is for the adolescent, because regardless of how minor any decision might be, the experience of being independent is what counts most in the adolescent's development. As the problems an adolescent faces become more complex, more serious, and have longer-lasting consequences, parents should play a more active role

in the decision-making process, not as a decision maker but
as a major *consultant*.

What courses youngsters will take in school, what colleges
to attend, who they should pal around with in high school,
parties they will go to, friends they will bring home, after-
school jobs they might take are typical issues that arise, and
in dealing with these issues the parent can offer recommendations. The adolescent needs and wants significant input
from parents, though the approach adolescents often use to
solicit advice can be misleading.

"Hey, Mom, *I'm going* to take a job as a waitress down at
X cocktail lounge on Saturday nights. The pay is good."

"You're going to do what?"

"I told you, a waitress."

"You will not. You won't dare. I catch you working down
at that place, and I'll haul you out. Over my dead body a
daughter of mine will work there. What's gotten into you?"

It's very easy to jump down the throat of an adolescent
who casually introduces a proposal of future plans or informs
the parents of some already acted-out behavior. The fact that
the adolescent makes an opener is indicative that he or she is
seeking a parent's response.

"I think I'm going to X college. A lot of kids I know are
going there."

"X college! That's no place for you."

Having a pat answer, a ready "no," is enough to turn the
adolescent off, and rightly so. The consultant role is one of
reasoning, volunteering opinions, providing foresight about
possible consequences.

No one likes to be told what to do. Adolescents aren't
unique in this respect. We all like to think we are responsible
for our own choices. Shouting threats won't deter an adolescent from going ahead with plans, but spending time and

energy as a consultant *can* make a difference.

A father of a teenage son who had recently learned to drive was concerned about his son driving home from parties where he might have had a beer or something stronger. His son couldn't see how one drink could affect him.

"I knew I couldn't stop him. If he was going to drink, he was going to drink. I wasn't going to be at the party. He told me all the kids drink and nothing happens. Maybe I used scare tactics," the father admitted. "I had to give the kid evidence." The father obtained film strips used in some driver education classes showing every conceivable kind of accident which was the result of the influence of alcohol. "All I could do was ask him to look at the films and make his decision. He watched. He didn't say a word. I told him I had a cousin killed in a car accident; the other guy was drunk." The father wondered if he had gone too far. However, when the son told him "Okay, I got the point," the father recognized he had achieved his goal without getting into a battle.

When your adolescent faces important, complicated decisions with potentially serious, long-term consequences, be sure you make clear the realistic limits within which any decision must be made. In your role as a major consultant, provide whatever information, opinions, and advice you can, but remain in the role of consultant; don't take over your adolescent's responsibility for the final decision making.

In discussing the general issue of realistic limits with parents, we are often asked what the limits should be in any given instance. Frankly, we cannot offer any general list of limits that would make sense and fit every situation. So much depends upon the particular situation and the people who are involved. Nevertheless, we believe it is very helpful for parents to stand back from the immediate problem and consider what they can afford (if money is involved), what they can accept and live with. Remember that the adolescent needs some structure, some clearcut boundaries within which he or she can make choices and decisions. It is important that these boundaries be as reasonable as possible from both the adolescent's and parent's points of view, but it is even more important that the boundaries be clearly communicated and understood.

We have found that many problems are avoided once an adolescent knows and understands the clearcut limits within which he or she can make personal choices. All too often, an adolescent's transgression of limits stems from a parent's failure to convey clearly and unequivocally what the parent views as realistic and reasonable boundaries of behavior. However, it may also be important for the parent to make equally clear the consequences of an adolescent exceeding explicit limits. These consequences must not be conveyed as threats or warnings, but rather as matter-of-fact results of going beyond rational limits of behavior. Once again, we cannot offer any general list of consequences that would fit every situation, but far more important than any specific consequences is the process of both parent and adolescent considering, openly and together, the reasonable limits within which they can live, and the rational consequences of exceeding these limits.

When it comes to decisions that many parents consider to be critical in the lives of their youngsters, decisions about sex, drugs, alcohol, and other similar matters, parental advice isn't resisted as much as parents might think. The experiences are new, and the adolescent might be feeling some conflict or confusion. Unfortunately, the emotional overtones surrounding these issues are so strong that parents either want to escape and close their eyes, hoping the issue will disappear, or they go overboard and explode. The first time a youngster comes home and by hints or indiscretions reveals an experience with pot or some other drug, most parents are shaken.

"Serve as a consultant!" scoffed one parent after learning her daughter had tried pot. "Reason with that fool daughter of mine? You spend all those years thinking you're being a good parent, and the kid comes home and drops something like this in your lap. I'll be damned if I talk to her as if she were adult."

But this is precisely the time when an adolescent needs parental advice, support, and counseling *without* histrionics. One mother who thought she was being very modern reported that when her daughter revealed an experience with pot she made a point of not reacting. "I shrugged my shoulders and wouldn't comment. I thought I was being very smart, not making an issue about pot." Much to her surprise her daughter kept at her, reminding her of her experience, giving hints about future experimentation. After a while it dawned on the mother that her daughter was getting angry because she *wasn't* reacting. Her daughter assumed that her mother's outwardly casual manner was real indifference about her welfare.

"I got the feeling she wanted me to get upset. She wanted me to do something to make her stop before she went too far."

We all need significant others in our lives who care about what we do. Adolescence perhaps more than any other time in life is surrounded with feelings of "No one loves me. I don't count. I'm not really anybody." Adolescents welcome a rediscovery of the fact that their parents do care and care enough to say, in effect, "Okay, you're older now. You're

going to do things I don't like to see you do. At least hear me
out and know that I care.'' Instead of fighting against an
adolescent's decision, instead of trying to hand out orders,
the parent who serves as a major consultant in the adolescent's decision making will probably have a much greater
impact on the adolescent's decisions and will strengthen,
rather than weaken, their relationship.

*Make every effort not to magnify the possible dangers
your teenager might face, and don't exaggerate, either
to yourself or to your adolescent, the long-term importance of any decision. Learn to respect your adolescent's
strengths, abilities, and resilience, and remember that
your adolescent is likely to show the greatest psychological growth in responding to real problems and real
difficulties which the adolescent feels honestly and
legitimately responsible for resolving.*

As adolescents grow older and assume more and more
responsibility for decisions affecting their lives, the relationship between parent and teenager should gradually grow into an interaction between mutually concerned but independent adults. Obviously, that is the aim of every parent, but it
can be achieved only if parents recognize, appreciate, and
respect the adolescent's need for the chance to make independent choices.

It is impossible to specify either the rate at which every
adolescent should assume independent responsibility or the
degree to which every parent should be involved in particular decisions. However, in this regard, parents should
remember the general principle that during the period in
which their children are adolescents, it is almost always
better to *under*parent than to *over*parent when it comes to
making choices and decisions directly concerned with the
teenager's life.

Nothing can substitute for first-hand experience, and parents must realize that they are doing a disservice to their teenagers by trying to protect them from facing the difficulties and problems of the real world. Adolescents frequently display their greatest spurts in psychological growth as a result of encountering problems which they are responsible for solving, even if they make some mistakes and get into some difficult situations because of decisions they have made. If adolescents feel honestly responsible for their own choices and decisions, they are most likely to respond to problems actively and energetically, sometimes making mistakes, as everyone does, but more importantly, developing into mature, well-integrated, effectively functioning adults as a result of these teenage opportunities.

Guidelines for Rational Parenting

Rational parenting involves more than passively allowing your adolescent to become independent; it means actively fostering, encouraging, and rewarding your adolescent's growing independence.

To achieve this goal you must identify those areas of your adolescent's life in which it is reasonable to expect independent choices and decisions. As a first step, consider your adolescent's day-to-day life and list the various choices and decisions that must be made. Begin with the most common daily events—what time to get up in the morning, what to eat for breakfast, when to leave for school—and then add to the list those issues that don't occur daily but nevertheless require some decisions, for example, choosing clothes or planning what to do during a vacation. Be as specific as you can, and think of each of these instances as potential opportunities for your adolescent to practice becoming independent.

Now, review this lit of possibilities with your adolescent

and add to the list the opportunities for independence that your adolescent thinks of in the course of your discussion. At this point, keep your discussion focused on the task of constructing a comprehensive list of opportunities for independence; don't be concerned about who should be involved and how each decision should be made.

With your adolescent, go through each of the possibilities you have listed and consider how the decisions are made at the present time. Then, viewing each item on the list as a potential opportunity for practicing independence, consider ways in which the range of independent decisions your adolescent makes can be expanded. For example, if you are now primarily responsible for making decisions about what clothes to buy for your adolescent, how can your adolescent assume greater independent responsibility in making these choices?

As you work together on this task, you may very well encounter some disagreements. After all, any judgment about who should make any particular decision depends upon one's point of view. You and your adolescent certainly have somewhat different perspectives and thus view the world differently, so some disagreement is to be expected. Face these disagreements together—agreeing that disagreement is all right—and jointly work towards a compromise that both of you can live with. Whenever possible, and in every instance that is reasonable to you, move towards increasing those areas of life in which your adolescent can become more independent.

Recognize that for all of us, independence is not a matter of all or none; independence and interdependence must be balanced. The task is not so much one of identifying possibilities for complete independence, but rather of adjusting the balance between dependence and interdependence in order to further maturity.

Having come to joint decisions together, stick to your agreements. There is nothing more important for rational parenting than being consistent. However, from time to time review your agreements together and readjust the balance between independence and interdependence to make it fit your adolescent's growing maturity.

Limits, Privileges, and Responsibilities

When it comes to limits, privileges, and responsibilities, be firm, fair, explicit, and consistent.

"Where are you going?"

"Out."

"In the car?"

"Of course in the car. Remember, I got my driver's license."

"Where are you taking the car?"

We stumbled around with further questions. One of our children had been a fully licensed driver for twenty-four hours. During the learning period when we sat alongside of him, trembling at every turn, smashing our feet against the floor board depressing imaginary brakes, we hadn't really believed the day would come when he would be driving alone. Wasn't it just yesterday he was on a bike with training wheels? Of course, he took driver's education; of course, we added countless scraps of advice. But all that is different from an actual solo, a day we weren't too eager to face.

In the American culture, the closest ceremony we have to a rite of passage into adulthood is getting a driver's license. Having a license and using the family car are, however, quite different issues. And so the first day after our son obtained his license, we were ready to challenge his going any further than the learning process. We had all sorts of reasons why he should stay home. It was raining; the car needed gas; it wasn't a good idea to drive at night. For each stumbling block he had a ready answer. He would use his allowance to buy gas; he couldn't drive only on bright, sunny days; he had already had experience driving at night with us.

With last minute shouted precautions, enough to unnerve an experienced driver, we returned to the house for the vigil. Few parents can leave the house comfortably the first time an adolescent takes the car. We spent a restless night waiting. Every time the telephone rang, we jumped, expecting the worst. For most parents sitting and waiting is a torture because they aren't sure about that first solo flight.

At twelve our son wasn't home; we had more black coffee. At two he still hadn't returned, and we debated calling the police. At four we were still around the kitchen table, our tension mounting. At six we decided to call the police. We had a small reserve of hope that nothing serious had happened. Wouldn't we have been telephoned? At 6:30 the car appeared in one piece in the driveway with our son gripping the wheel, sitting in that upright position of stiff attention characteristic of new drivers.

"Where the hell have you been?"

During the long hours of waiting, we had been sentimental. If only we could see him and know he was all right, we would be grateful. When he did appear and was all right, sentiment fled, and all we could do was lash out in fury.

"Give us the keys to the car. It's the last time you get the car. Where the hell is your sense of responsibility? What do you mean by keeping us up all night?"

A steady stream of abuse. Doors slamming; chairs kicked over; "Get out of this house"; a suitcase being packed, tears.

"Won't you listen to my side of the story?" our son asked.

"There isn't another side." We told him of our desperation and worry.

"But I was all right."

"How did we know you were okay?"

"What did you think happened?"

"Plenty." We hesitated going over our fantasies. "Why didn't you call? Why didn't you let us know?" We had countless why's.

His story was uncomplicated. He had been at a party. At two he fully expected to get in the car and drive home; however, he had been very sleepy and got worried about driving. He went back into the house and thought that if he took a nap for a few minutes he'd be okay and ready to drive home. He, too, had been shocked to realize it was morning. It had crossed his mind that we might be worried, but since he was fine, he couldn't see any reason why we were worried.

According to him we shouldn't have stayed up all night. Why hadn't we gone to bed? Our panic, our fears, our near hysteria at his not returning the entire night were incomprehensible.

Make sure that you and your adolescent know what to expect from each other, what is acceptable and what is not acceptable.

The mistake was ours. Although we had bombarded him with all sorts of driving advice prior to his leaving, we hadn't said anything about a curfew time. A lot of anxiety on our part could have been saved if we had made the ground rules explicit. We finally convinced him that our feelings of concern, justified or not, had been very real. We told him that it was only fair that in return for using the car he had certain limits and responsibilities. All we wanted was some idea of where he was going and the approximate time we might expect him to return. If for any reason he was delayed or something unexpected occurred, would he call us? The hour didn't matter. The rule, he agreed, was reasonable. We, in turn, were going to be saved from another sleepless night.

The following Saturday evening he again took the car. "Don't worry," he said with a sly smile, "I got your message." Starting at eight, telephone calls came in regularly every half hour. At the fifth call, when our favorite TV program was again interrupted, even we relented and called a halt to the checking in.

It's hard for an adolescent on his or her way to independence to realize the depth of parental concern. They are often too wrapped up in themselves to really stop and take another's perspective, particularly if that other person is a parent. More often than not this is a time of self-worry, self-concern, self-interest, and adolescents may even bask in their own feelings of "Nobody cares about me, no one loves me, I don't count for much."

Frances, a seventeen-year-old, talked about how jarred she felt when she realized how much her mother cared. She realized she had taken her mother's concern as a matter of course. "Maybe it's because she only shows it by having me do something all the time or telling me what to do that I never think about it."

The recognition of her mother's interest—"almost as if I saw for the first time how much I meant"—came when Frances failed to return home from a date until early in the morning. Her mother was waiting up for her; when Frances opened the door, the first greeting was a strong slap across her face. "I was ready to leave home. I told my mother if she ever hit me again I would hit her back and walk out. She didn't even hear me. She started crying. I never saw her cry like that. I ended up comforting her."

Frances' mother told her daughter how much she had worried, how distraught she had been because Frances failed to come home at a reasonable hour. She had imagined horrible things happening; and when Frances finally appeared, she had lost control of herself—"worry, anger, and relief" was how she put it. Frances promised that from then on she would call her mother if she was going to be later than usual. "We were a lot closer after that. I kept my promise. She told me she just likes to know what I'm doing and that I'm safe."

Work out your adolescent's privileges, limits, and responsibilities together rather than imposing your expectations on your teenagers.

Peggy's announcement that she had volunteered their home for a party threw her mother into a panic. Her first thoughts were about potential disasters—a messy kitchen, wrecked living room. The concern wasn't completely unrealistic. Many parents share the same fears. In fact, when she had asked her daughter why the party couldn't be held elsewhere, her daughter's response was "None of the other parents will let the kids have a party. They're scared of what happens."

"It was all right for other parents to say no, but my daugher is the one to say 'Sure, have the party at my house.' "

Rather than gamble on Peggy's assurance that the party wouldn't wreck the house, her mother suggested that Peggy and several of the party organizers get together to talk about the plans. One afternoon the youngsters met and Peggy's mother went over her concerns and asked the teenagers to suggest how problems might be handled. What to do about smoking, drinking, cleaning up at the end of the party, and keeping out unwanted guests were a few of the issues she raised. She was surprised to discover that in many instances the youngsters were tougher about how they might cope with problems than she would have been if faced with the same situations. For example, she didn't want smoking of any sort in the house. Peggy didn't smoke, but she knew others in the group did. "What are you going to do with smokers—pot, cigarettes, or anything?"

"Kick them out of the party," said one adolescent.

"How are you going to do that?" Peggy's mother had visions of going up to a seventeen-year-old who was smoking and asking him to leave the party.

"No sweat," said one of the boys. "You get a few guys. You pick up the smoker and throw him out."

The solutions the adolescents offered were straightforward. "If you don't want kids drinking liquor," one boy advised, "get rid of the bottles. Put them in a closet."

The youngsters didn't want adults visible. Peggy's mother agreed to stay away from the house for the early part of the evening. When she returned, the compromise was she would remain out of sight, but if matters got out of hand, she would exercise her right to interfere without hard feelings.

Not one of the youngsters rebelled at Peggy's mother's limits. In return for the privilege of having the party they were able to work out solutions. It would have been easier in the long run to have refused to let the party take place. Through sharing her concerns, enlisting the support and advice of the adolescents, she achieved her goal—a safe party, without damage to the house and, as it turned out, a good time for the youngsters who attended.

Many parents have problems establishing and maintaining limits with their adolescents. They may be unclear about what the limits are or inconsistent in keeping to the limits already established. They may not even be sure themselves about what limits are reasonable and as a result be unrealistically severe. Just as a problem might occur from undue severity about limits, difficulty might have occurred with overindulgence. Parents may feel that imposing limits on their adolescents is somehow a sign of lack of affection, and to prove their parental love, both to themselves and to others, they try to gratify any wish or whim that their adolescents might have.

Being afraid to cross one's adolescent is not an unusual trap for parents to get caught up in. Many parents who have discussed this problem with us say they are frightened that their youngster will do something harmful to themselves and in turn hurt their parents. They point to horror stories of other people's children who, when restricted, openly defied their parents with some act that seriously hurt their lives.

From a developmental point of view the issue of limits is especially significant during adolescence. The teenager is living through a time of tremendous growth and development, with important physical changes as well as changes in personal and social expectations. Adolescence is normally a period of some psychological instability, some disequilibrium, irresolution, wavering, hesitation, and restlessness.

Although this instability may very well be uncomfortable for both the adolescent and the parent, at this stage of life it is psychologically healthy and desirable because it serves as a developmental bridge from childhood to young adulthood. If the adolescent were to remain entirely stable and steady throughout the teenage years, there would be little opportunity for the kind of psychological growth that is necessary in changing from child to young adult.

Given the normal, necessary, desirable, and healthy internal instability of adolescence, the need for a stable, well-structured, predictable external world is even greater at this stage of development than at most other times in life. Therefore, for the sake of teenagers' own sense of security as

well as the peace of mind of their parents, it is especially important for adolescents to know exactly what is expected of
them and the limits of behavior that are acceptable to
others. And it is equally important for parents to make clear
and explicit the consequences of exceeding or transgressing
these acceptable limits. As we have said earlier, we cannot list
the appropriate consequences of breaking acceptable limits
because so much depends upon the particular circumstances
of a specific incident. But we wish to emphasize that what is
of the greatest importance in every case is the explicit mutual
understanding between parents and their adolescents.

When children are young, a good part of our communication consists of some form of guidance, establishing limits
or giving directives. "Don't go off the block; come right
home; eat your dinner; take a bath; do your homework; go
to bed." Few parents, if any, really can sit down with a small
child for a long, involved discussion about the rationale
behind expected behaviors. And certainly we don't turn to a
six-year-old or a ten-year-old for advice about the adult
world in which we are involved. So by the time our children
are adolescents we have a long backlog of experience in
manipulating, controlling, and imposing limits. It comes as
somewhat of a shock when we discover adolescents in our
house who don't bend easily to our demands, who won't
conform to our wishes, and who don't jump when a command is given. We all think it's cute when a four-year-old in
response to an order to go to bed asks "Why?" In fact, we
may even encourage the process of questioning in young
children. At that time in life we willingly talk about educational inquiry and feel good about giving answers to the
challenges preadolescents raise.

When children are adolescents and engage in the same
kind of questioning process, our blood pressure may rise.

"Why can't I stay up as long as I want to?" asks the adolescent. "Why can't I smoke pot?" "Why can't I have sex?" The relatively simple questions of childhood suddenly are complex and can't be dismissed with simple, shortcut answers. In many cases we may not even have a ready answer; our own lack of sureness makes us uncomfortable in being put on the spot. More often than not we react with irritation and annoyance.

"Why do I have to explain everything?" asked one father. "I am his parent. I pay the bills. As long as I support him and he lives at home, he damn well better listen." Parental power up until adolescence is strong, and power isn't easily given up, no more than authority is easily relinquished anywhere else in society. The transition from an authoritarian family style to a democratic relationship is a difficult move, particularly when the issues involved are more than simple challenges about how much TV can be watched or whether it's okay to have an extra dessert.

"Tell my daughter I don't want her sleeping with boys at her age?" said one father. He was angered that his fifteen-year-old daughter might have to be told this kind of fact. "I don't care what other girls her age do. That's their parents' concern. When it comes to Missy—all I can tell you is if she does, she's in real trouble with me."

"Have you told her how you feel?"

"Tell her? She knows. Does everything have to be spelled out?"

From the father's point of view nothing could have been more absurd, not to say embarrassing, than to sit down with his well-developed fifteen-year-old daughter for a discussion of sex and his reasons for not wanting her to have sexual relations with boys at this age.

A simple no won't work in adolescence, and this is often

troubling to parents. Just as a simple no won't achieve results, neither will threats about throwing them out of the house, screaming, or tears do the job. Parents often resent this, and thus there is a lot of discussion about being tyrannized by adolescents. The fact is that it isn't tyranny when parents offer reasonable explanations instead of straightforward nos or emotional scenes.

Firm, fair, explicit, consistent limits and expectations provide some of the external structure that adolescents need, and to a certain extent they also relieve some of the stress that parents usually experience during this period of parenthood.

In Missy's case her father did eventually talk with her, letting her know how disturbed he would be and sharing his concern about her and her relationships. Afterwards, he told us he felt relieved from the suspicion, anger, and stress he had been living with wondering about her behavior. From Missy's point of view, she, too, admitted relief. "I kind of didn't want to anyhow," she said. The fact that he had talked *with* her instead of *at* her served to accomplish his goal, and Missy felt a lot happier about herself.

In a major study of adolescents' conflicts with parents about limits, the principal areas reported were hours adolescents returned home at night, school performance, spending of money, choice of friends, and personal habits. In another important investigation of the qualities adolescents most wished in their parents, among the most-frequently-mentioned responses was their need for parents to respect their opinions.

Although studies suggest that there are a group of specific, concrete issues which seem to create the greatest sources of conflict between parents and adolescents, by no means do we suggest that these exhaust the range of issues an individual family faces. What is a problem for one family may not be an issue in another. What may be wrong in terms of limits for one family may be viewed as right or acceptable in another. Each family must work out among itself the kind of rules and expectations with which family members are most comfortable living. We do emphasize the idea of working out rules *together*. The results are always better when parent and adolescent jointly establish the limits of daily life and when each knows exactly what to expect from the other.

From time to time, review your expectations with your adolescent, and change your expectations to keep them in line with the teenager's increasing maturity.

Deciding upon fair and reasonable limits together doesn't mean that all problems in a given area will be resolved for the remainder of adolescence. Parents must expect their adolescent to test the limits once in a while; this is a normal part of growing up. In addition, as adolescents mature, the limits placed on them need to be revised and sometimes substantially changed. After all, one would hardly expect an eighteen-year-old to live within the same set of limits that would be reasonable at thirteen or fourteen. Testing the limits is one way of reminding the parent that no matter how fair and rational limits are at one age, they must be reconsidered and perhaps revised as the adolescent matures.

As an adolescent grows older, responsibilities and privileges should increase appropriately. Remember that responsibility stimulates psychological growth, but too much responsibility too soon in a person's life can be stifling and frustrating.

Be fair and flexible in making decisions about limits and responsibilities, but once these decisions are agreed upon, be consistent. Don't change your expectations arbitrarily. Remember that it is much more important to provide a stable, predictable environment for your adolescent than to appear to be benign but really be inconsistent.

Just as it is crucial for teenagers to be aware of the limits on their behavior, it is equally important for them to understand their privileges and responsibilities within the family. Privileges and responsibilities go together, and as an adolescent matures, these two aspects of daily living should be kept in balance. An adolescent with too many responsibilities feels frustrated and overburdened; an adolescent with too many privileges acquires an unrealistic view of life and is ill prepared to face the normal demands of young adulthood. Therefore, privileges and responsibilities must be kept in harmony with each other, both increasing as the adolescent moves toward adult status.

Guidelines for Rational Parenting

In making decisions about your adolescent's limits, privileges, and responsibilities, the way in which the decisions are made is as important as the decisions themselves. Instead of taking an authoritarian stance, making judgments that are "handed down from above," the rational parent involves the adolescent in the decision-making process. Thus, the likelihood that the adolescent will respect the limits and fulfill the responsibilities agreed upon is greatly enhanced. In this respect, adolescents are no different from adults; the greater our involvement in making a decision, the more likely we will follow through on that decision in our subsequent behavior. This does not mean that the parent abdicates a position of responsibility and authority, but it is a position of rational authority rather than authoritarianism.

Before involving your adolescent in decision-making processes, make sure you have clarified for yourself your own views about limits, privileges, and responsibilities. Clarification does not imply making hard and fast decisions, but it does mean being clear in your own mind about what you believe is reasonable and understanding the rational basis of your views. Therefore, as a first step, consider each of the following questions:

• What are the most important limits you have placed on your adolescent?

• What are the reasons for each of the limits you have placed on your adolescent?

• Do you and your adolescent disagree about these limits?

• What happens when you and your adolescent disagree about limits?

• What are the most important responsibilities you expect your adolescent to fulfill?

• What are the most important privileges you've given your adolescent?

• Do you and your adolescent disagree about privileges?

• What privilege does your adolescent want most that he or she doesn't have at the present time?

• What are the reasons for this decision?

After you have clarified your own point of view, ask your adolescent to consider these questions with you. In this discussion, make your own views explicit, but also work at understanding how your adolescent experiences these matters. This means following principles of rational parenting: listen without interrupting and without prejudging, and emphathize rather than analyze.

When you and your adolescent disagree, reason together in identifying the basis of your disagreement. Remember that the purpose of this discussion is to understand each other's point of view and to work out compromises that you are satisfied with and that your adolescent is satisfied with. You are not out to prove each other guilty or at fault, so avoid attacking your adolescent for previous behaviors. Don't get caught up in the blame game. If your adolescent feels threatened, gets defensive, and starts attacking you, don't respond with a counterattack. Instead, recognize that your adolescent is feeling threatened, and together try to understand the reasons for this feeling. Then, on the basis of this understanding work together to reduce this sense of threat so that the two of you can get on with the task of working out rational limits, privileges, and responsibilities.

Knowing the Right Situation for Each Adolescent

Encourage your adolescents to discover the kinds of situations in which they function most effectively and the kinds of people with whom they are most compatible.

Peter made the varsity swim squad in his freshman year in high school. Regardless of the weather, his mood, or physical condition, he went to practice. As the youngest member of the team, he was single-minded in his goal to turn in a good performance. There was only one problem. The coach was jarred by Peter's personality. Peter was talkative, eager, and excited. The coach made no secret of his preference for quiet, retiring youngsters who "jumped" at his every command.

As a result of the coach's intense dislike for Peter, he never wasted a moment to harass the youngster. Every performance was publicly criticized. He made an effort to have the rest of the team take action and vote Peter off the team.

Peter reported the coach's dislike to his parents. Their initial reaction was to encourage him to try harder. Their advice was partly due to old-fashioned notions that one doesn't quit, that one has to learn to get along with all kinds of authority figures. They also realized that Peter was an active youngster, and it was possible that his style rubbed the coach the wrong way.

Each day after practice Peter had another dismal tale to

relate about the coach's vendetta. In desperation, Peter's mother decided to talk to the coach. The decision wasn't easy. A parent goes to see an elementary teacher when there's a problem. Going to a high school teacher, the parents felt, posed the risk of embarrassing their son. However, in this case Peter's mother felt she had to check out some of her son's story, to find out for herself whether Peter's stories were true.

The interview convinced her that Peter's description of the situation was based on fact. As she recalled, ''When I asked him if he disliked Peter, he didn't answer me. The conversation wasn't solving anything. I wondered if I had made matters worse, but at least I knew Peter wasn't imagining what was going on.''

Psychologists, and parents as well, like to believe that teachers are special people who have learned to control their feelings and personal dislikes. In fact, this isn't always the case. In this instance Peter's staying in an impossible situation, despite the possible rewards of swimming success, was pointless. There is a time to stay with the impossible and there is a time to give it up. Peter had struggled to adapt to the coach for two seasons. The conditions weren't getting any better.

When adolescents are in the wrong situation, don't force them to beat their heads against a stone wall. Help them to change to a situation that is better suited to them.

The next time Peter talked about quitting the team, his parents supported the decision. They helped Peter understand that the coach's personal style was at odds with Peter's. Nothing he could do could change the coach's attitude. If Peter chose to remain in swimming, he had to accept the conditions.

Peter decided to leave the squad; he joined the cross country team instead. Aside from sporadic periods of jogging when trying to get in shape for swimming, Peter hadn't done much running; however, the track coach, a firm but kind man with extraordinary insight into adolescents, assured Peter that experience did not matter. What counted for this coach was eagerness, enthusiasm, and involvement.

Peter plunged into track with the same kind of fiery energy he had put into swimming. He ran whether there was snow, mud, rain, or fog. His parents attended the final meet of the season and watched their son lead the pack in the final cross country event. The coach talked with them and said how impressed he was with Peter's intensity and spirited approach to life. He particularly admired Peter's perserverance and ability to work hard. The same youngster had been seen through completely different lenses. In the evaluation of one coach, Peter had been an irritating adolescent; in the opinion of another, Peter was a hard worker, an exciting addition to the team. The right mix in personal styles made all the difference.

Just as each of us has particular talents and skills that influence the nature of our achievements, so too there are particular situations in which each of us functions best. Some do best in large groups, with lots of social interaction and a high level of stimulation. Others do best when they are alone or with one or two others, in a quiet environment with a low level of external stimulation. Similarly, there are certain kinds of people with whom each of us can get along, although we have difficulty relating to others. And all of us differ from one another in our preferences.

In short, there are *right* and there are *wrong* situations for each of us. If we are in a situation that is right for us, we are much more likely to feel comfortable, to be productive, and to achieve at a level that fits our talents. And if we are in a situation that is wrong for us, we are probably much less comfortable and much less likely to fulfill our talents. No matter how flexible or how adaptable we might be, the situations we live and work in make a difference in how well we function.

Choosing the right situations and being fortunate or skilled enough to achieve our goals is a large part of successful living. As adults most of us have some degree of freedom in choosing the people with whom we interact most and the kinds of situations in which we spend much of our time. Obviously, these choices are limited for everyone. No one is entirely free. All of us have duties and obligations we cannot escape. All of us must deal with situations that make us uncomfortable or may be downright unpleasant and certainly not self-fulfilling, and everyone must get along with some people we would much rather avoid altogether. No one lives in the *right* situation with the *right* people all the time. Nevertheless, an adult usually has some choice in these matters, and whether or not we are aware of our preferences, within the practical limits of our everyday lives we tend to choose the situations that fit us best.

Adolescents have a much narrower range of choices. Until very late adolescence they are required to go to school, and in school they must deal with classroom situations over which they have little control and perhaps little or no voice in choosing. A large part of the curriculum they must study is determined by other people whom they have never met or even seen and who know nothing about them as individuals. And frequently the teachers they must work with are assigned by some administrative decision rather than chosen by the teenager.

Help your adolescents learn that success depends not

only on their talents and skills, but also on how well
they fit with the demands of a particular situation and
the personal style of other people.

Sue felt she deserved a part in the school's annual musical. "Everyone said I should have gotten a part. I have one of the best voices. You can ask anyone." She accused the teacher of being unfair.

Sue had an excellent singing voice. She had dramatic ability, and the youngsters chosen for the major roles were, in her father's opinion, far less talented. He wondered whether personal bias was keeping his daughter from success.

However, he ultimately took an objective view of the situation. Sue's father helped her think through the reasons why she might not have gotten a part. What were the unwritten rules for getting roles? It turned out that principal parts were traditionally given to seniors. In addition, the theater director had said that all the students who wanted roles had to put in time working back stage. Sue had not fulfilled these conditions. She was extremely talented, but in the school setting there were rules which had to be followed.

Outside of school, the situation was different. Sue joined a theatrical group in the community and won a part, so instead of remaining frustrated in a situation at school that was wrong for her, Sue found another situation that was better suited to her talents and allowed her to experience some success.

School represents only one part of our adolescent's life, and perhaps in other aspects of daily living an adolescent's choices may not be so restricted. Nevertheless, in comparison to most adults, the majority of adolescents have a much more restricted range of choices with regard to both situations and people.

Even with these restrictions, parents can help their adolescents understand and appreciate the importance of situational factors in achieving their goals. To get along in the world, obviously, the adolescent cannot expect to live and work only in situations that fit them perfectly; they must learn to adapt to a variety of situations and to different kinds of people. Developing some flexibility, therefore, is crucial for an adolescent's growth. Naturally, some situations are more interesting, more comfortable, more apt to result in productivity than others. And some people are more congenial and compatible than others.

This may seem to be a rather obvious idea that everyone should be aware of and that should need no special attention, but the egocentric perspective of adolescents often obscures the importance of anything other than themselves. When they achieve success, they are likely to assume that their success depended entirely on their own performance; and when they experience failure, they may very well feel that it was a result only of their own personal inadequacies. In either case, the importance of the adolescent's interaction with the situation and with other people is forgotten, neglected, or misunderstood. Thus, adolescents need to be shaken from their largely egocentric stance, and they need to learn that both success and failure depend not only on their own talents and skills but also on how well their talents and skills fit the demands of a given situation and how well their personal style fits the styles of others in that situation. Teenagers have to learn how to see the world in interactional terms, rather than from their own egocentric perspective. Because of their preoccupation with themselves, they frequently lose sight of even the simplest and most obvious facts about the world, such as the fact that the situation makes a difference. Parents, therefore, can serve an important function in their teenagers' psychological development by reminding them of this basic fact of life.

Although awareness of the fact that the situation makes a difference can be reassuring to teenagers, general insights about living are never very meaningful until they are brought down to the concrete realities of a person's everyday life. Parents must therefore help their adolescents move beyond the knowledge of a general principle to an awareness of the particular kinds of situations in which they function most effectively.

Gaining this awareness is not always an easy process. It demands a self-examination of one's own trials and errors, identifying the situations in which one has succeeded and those in which one has failed, and this process can be emotionally stressful. It requires some degree of objectivity in reflecting about one's own past performance. Especially difficult is the task of facing failures coolly, rationally, objectively. All of us tend to forget our less successful efforts in life, and when we do examine them we are likely to distort our recall of what happened. Given the normal self-concern of adolescence, we can expect a certain amount of defensiveness when teenagers face their past failures.

Teenagers' defensiveness can be reduced if parents make it abundantly clear that the process of self-examination should be aimed at identifying the situational factors associated with success and failure, *not* at assigning blame either to the teenager or to others. In the course of a teen's self-examination, parents can be most helpful to them by carefully and consistently maintaining an objective, totally nonblaming stance. If parents can remain rational and non-threatening in their discussions with their teenagers about past achievements, past frustrations, difficulties, and failures, there is a much greater chance that the teenagers themselves will be less defensive.

Help your adolescents face the facts of their past successes and failures, and thus learn from their own experiences about the kind of situations in which they function most effectively and with the greatest satisfaction.

Insight, of course, is not enough. Merely recognizing that certain situations are right for them and others are wrong may relieve some of the pressure adolescents feel when they encounter difficulties, but they must move beyond understanding to action. They must learn to avoid as best they can the kinds of situations in which they don't fit well and the kinds of people with whom their own personal styles clash. This isn't always possible, however, and an important aspect of maturity is learning to adapt to situations and to other people even when the "mix" is not personally optimal. But parents should not be rigid in insisting that their adolescents adapt to every situation regardless of how bad the mix might be. When a teenager runs into difficulties, parents must be sensitive to the possibility that these difficulties stem from an unfortunate interaction between the teenager and a particular situation.

For years we had managed a children's camp. It was a perfect place for Nancy, a teenage friend of ours. A leader, outstanding in every activity, she had been an ideal camper as a child. However, when she reached adolescence, the same situation in which she had achieved such outstanding success and rewards was now all wrong.

We remember the disaster of her fifteenth summer. Our "honor camper" was impossible to control. The other adolescents were doing fine. Nancy was the only one upsetting routines, devising pranks, and defying rules. We spent considerable time giving Nancy inspirational talks about getting back on the track, becoming once again the out-standing, dependable girl we had known in the past. The promises to start over lasted until we were out of earshot.

The situation at the time was wrong for Nancy. She wanted to be home that summer working, making new friends. Her parents had resisted. Her father had just started a new business, and her mother planned on helping her husband. He needed her in the office to answer telephones and mail. Without family responsibilities at home, Nancy's mother would feel free to accompany her husband to the office and remain all day. If Nancy remained at home, they faced a problem. There wouldn't be an adult around during the day and on many an evening to provide supervision. Without school to take up her time, they were concerned that the days would be long; afternoons would drag and there were concerns about Nancy being at a loss about how to fill her time. The impulsive decision was one they felt everyone would regret. There were no guarantees friends would be around. As far as a job was concerned they knew from talking with other parents how difficult, almost im-possible, it was for a youngster Nancy's age to find regular employment.

We finally convinced them that at this stage in Nancy's life the situation, not Nancy, was at fault. Nancy left camp in the middle of the season. She spent the rest of her summer work-ing at a drive-in, loafing, and getting involved with new ac-tivities and friends. She admitted to being bored a lot of the time, but the situation where she could be bored had been her decision. What was wrong from her parents' perspective turned out to be exactly right for Nancy's development.

Guidelines for Rational Parenting
Although you cannot tell your adolescent what situations are

right for him or her, you can help in the process of self-discovery. But remember that you are the consultant, the sympathetic, interested helper in the process, not the teacher or the authority who knows what the right answer must be.

One way to help your adolescent begin this process of discovery is to suggest that for everyone—not just for adolescents—some situations fit better than others. This doesn't mean that we should always avoid or try to escape situations that we find difficult for us. All of us have to learn how to function under a variety of conditions and with various kinds of people. However, it is equally important to recognize that some kinds of situations are better for each of us than are others. For example, some people feel most comfortable and function most effectively when the demands of a situation are clearly structured and there is a clearcut hierarchy of responsibility. Other people prefer a situation which is more open, less structured and defined. But what situation is right for your adolescent? Obviously, there is no single answer that suits everyone. Therefore, the rational parent encourages the adolescent to discover the answer that fits best for him or her.

The best guide in this process of self-discovery is your adolescent's emotional reactions in various situations encountered in the past. The most useful clues are not necessarily the adolescent's history of achievement or any other external measure, but rather the adolescent's feelings.

An effective way of going about this process of self-discovery involves using a critical-incident technique. Ask your adolescent to think of critical incidents, particular times and situations in which he or she has felt comfortable, lively, interested, productive, enthusiastic; then, identify the common threads that run through these positive experiences.

What characteristics did these situations share? What was it that led to your adolescent's positive reactions?

Using the same critical-incident technique, you can think together about situations that were boring, uncomfortable, tense, threatening. What are the common characteristics shared by these negatively-toned situations? How do they differ from those that were viewed positively?

The answer to the basic question of what situations are best for your adolescent won't necessarily appear automatically or at once. But by working at the problem together, by following your adolescent's lead, you will both gain a much greater understanding of this entire issue.

Each Person's Talents

Encourage adolescents to
discover their own particular talents and
to set achievement goals that fit these talents.

Professional football teams have players whose only job is to kick the ball; the medical profession has doctors who treat only the ear or the eye; construction companies have carpenters who build only stairways. Specialization characterizes the work of almost all adults, not only football players, doctors, and carpenters. Each of us develops a limited range of skills, and we earn our living, contribute to society, achieve status and security largely on the basis of these particular skills.

But for one reason or another, the right to specialization that characterizes the adult world is sometimes denied adolescents. They are expected to be generalists whose achievement is measured across the board, assuming a homogeneity of talents that contrasts sharply with the more specialized skills expected of adults. Consider, for example, the grade average, which is the most commonly used measure of a student's academic achievement. Grades in mathematics, English, physics, shop, music, French, and almost anything else the student has enrolled in are lumped together, and by some simple arithmetic the student is assigned a single number that presumably represents "level of achievement." The student may be a brilliant mathematician, a marvelous musician, or a very gifted mechanic, but if the overall grade average is below a given point, that student is labeled a "low achiever."

By this standard almost all adults would be considered low achievers. A skillful surgeon we know is hopelessly inept when it comes to fixing his car or repairing the plumbing; a friend of ours who is an extraordinarily gifted musician would no doubt flunk most tests in high school math or history; a successful local banker confesses nearly total ignorance of American poetry, modern painting, and popular music. If these adults were evaluated in the same way adolescents are, their grade averages would certainly be low enough to stamp all of them as low achievers.

We are not arguing against the value of general knowledge and the desirability of developing a wide range of skills and interests. Our surgeon friend would undoubtedly be very happy if he could occasionally do some minor repairs on a car that seems to spend most of its time in a garage. The musician would probably be a more informed citizen if he knew a little more history, and our banker's life would certainly be enriched by some greater familiarity with the arts. But at this point we are concerned with one of the central issues of adolescence, the evaluation of achievement, and in this respect there is a clearcut discontinuity between adolescence and adult life. Adults are expected to specialize, and their achievements are viewed in terms of particular accomplishments. Adolescents, on the other hand, are expected to be generalists whose achievements are viewed in terms of a grade point average or the equivalent.

Teenagers with very unusual talents may escape the demand for general achievement. The rare musical genius of fifteen is not expected to be an outstanding basketball player; and the star of the basketball team is not expected to be a great mathematician. But these are exceptions. The vast majority of adolescents who are not blessed with extraordinary talents face the demands of a culture that evaluates teenage achievement primarily in general terms.

Underlying our reluctance to foster specialized talents in adolescence is the tendency in our society to prolong childhood. For a variety of reasons, the age at which an individual is expected to assume the responsibilities of adulthood has been getting later and later. This is partly because our society is becoming increasingly complex, and it simply takes longer to acquire all the skills necessary to deal with these complexities. Growing up in rural America a hundred years ago demanded certain skills and knowledge that a person might reasonably acquire at a minimal level by the age of fifteen. Thus, a fifteen-year-old could begin assuming certain adult responsibilities and be viewed more as an adult than a child. In our current, largely urban society, there is much more to learn, many more skills that are necessary to acquire, and so it takes longer to reach the point at which one is truly more of an adult than a child. As a result, the period of relatively childlike status has been extended.

Unfortunately, we often overdo our prolongation of childhood. We continue to view adolescents as relatively more childlike than adultlike for longer than the actual demands of our society require. And part of the price that is paid for this unrealistic extension of childhood is a failure to recognize and fully appreciate the unique talents of the individual teenager. In treating adolescents as childlike, we encourage a homogeneous pablum of achievement and foster the myth that the talents of one teenager are pretty much like those of every other teenager.

For some adolescents this leads to a sense of being locked into a straitjacket of conventional, across-the-board achievement. They feel that they cannot afford to pursue in depth a particular line of interest, develop a limited set of skills, satisfy their own idiosyncratic curiosities, and fulfill their own individual talents.

We faced this conflict with our son when he was sixteen. He had inherited an inexpensive guitar from an older brother, and at the time we thought a few lessons and several imperfectly learned songs would satisfy his musical interest and save our ears. Much to our dismay, his interest in the guitar increased. With savings from working at a part-time job plus advances from future birthday and holiday presents, he invested in an expensive guitar, which we mistakenly assumed would stay under his bed, a favorite storage place for various discarded interests.

This did not happen. Not only was the guitar used, but books, instruction manuals, and song sheets were bought with alarming frequency. He plucked away in the morning before school. After school, he again was at the guitar. We say "at" because much of what he was doing didn't sound very much like music to us.

Initially, we were patient, thinking his devotion and interest would wane in a few months. Instead, his attention to the guitar stepped up; the "real" things in life—history, calculus, chemistry, English—were shoved aside. His grades, the measure of an adolescent's academic worth, took a downward tumble, and the guitar playing, which hardly ranked high in our system of values to say nothing of the school's, spiraled upward.

"Isn't it great," he asked us one evening as he prepared to give his nightly serenade, "how much I've improved?"

Ignoring the agony reflected on our faces, he continued. "Didn't you think that last song was good?"

"How's French going?"

"I've improved a lot."

"That's not what the report said."

"I know the song by heart."

"Yes, but have you done your French homework?"

Evening after evening we were miserable, listening to the sounds of guitar playing coming from behind his closed bedroom door. On nights when we knew there was a test at school the next day, we felt even worse.

"Are you studying for the test?" Our light-hearted tone hardly masked the anxiety we were experiencing.

"You really hate me playing the guitar," he commented.

He was right on target. We hated the guitar. We resented every moment he "wasted" playing the instrument. Strumming the guitar *after* he had done his regular work made sense to us, and we probably would have been willing to serve as an appreciative audience then. But playing the guitar *instead* of doing homework assignments was downright stupid as far as his grades were concerned.

We worried that he might imagine himself as a future Segovia, his current hero at the time. Segovia probably didn't have to worry about grades during adolescence. Our son did, if he was going to achieve at school and get into college. We tried some subtle, underhanded tactics.

"You know," we casually told him, "taking up a musical career beyond eight or ten years of age is really impossible. Great musicians are always child prodigies. That's the way it is with music. Well, son, how about studying French and calculus more seriously?"

The oblique tactic didn't work. We went directly to the point. Damn it, if you spent as much time on your school work as you *waste* on the guitar playing, do you realize how great a student you could be?

The school supported our belief that too much attention to a guitar was ruining what really counted in the long run— achievement and good grades. Bluntly put, guitar playing wouldn't prepare him for life nor help him earn a living.

We withheld all praise, all encouragement, all rewards concerning his current affair with the guitar. We successfully managed to escape listening to home recitals. However, one day much later, we were caught unaware. He was playing; the house was quiet at the time. The guitar sounded quite good. In fact, he wasn't playing badly at all. Reluctantly, we gave a few words of praise. "Jeff, you played that song really well. It wasn't bad at all. We'll listen to it again if you want to play it over." Cautious about letting him get the wrong idea, we hurriedly added, "Just once, though, because we know you want to do your homework before it's too late."

Be sure your adolescent knows that everyone has different talents and that a person achieves most effectively when these talents are used.

It would probably be unwise for an adolescent to disregard entirely our society's demands for general achievement. However, some of the frustration that results from this demand can be tempered if the adolescent learns that each of us has certain, quite limited talents, and we achieve most effectively and usually with greatest personal satisfaction when we use those talents. This is the principal message about talent and achievement that parents must communicate to their adolescents, and if the communication is to have any meaningful impact, it must be followed up by the parents' genuine appreciation of their adolescent's particular talents.

Encourage your adolescent to discover his or her special talents, but recognize that discovering one's own talents requires some trial and error, and help your adolescent realize that making some mistakes in the process of self-discovery is perfectly normal.

Discovering one's own talents inevitably takes some trial

and error. No one is born knowing his or her special abilities. They must be discovered through experience. Our son never became a professional guitarist, though he admitted that he'd thought about it.

"What was so wrong with that fantasy?" he asked. "I learned a lot. I did it on my own. Just because I don't make a living at it doesn't mean I can't enjoy playing." These kinds of flirtations with fantasies had been so important, and yet we, like so many parents, forgetting our own dreams at this age, had not missed one opportunity to make sure our child approached life sensibly, practically, with two feet on the ground—and in the process attempted to shortchange the rewards of pursuing his own star.

From a psychological point of view, the opportunity to try yourself out in various activities and in different situations, with the freedom to make some errors along the way, is an essential part of an adolescent's development into maturity.

Tim excelled in science. He did average work in English, languages, and history. In math and chemistry he completed several experiments, applied for a summer program for gifted science students, and won a scholarship. At the last minute Tim told his father he had changed his plans. Instead of spending his summer vacation studying science, he wanted to join a theater group which was giving a series of productions in a resort community nearby.

Until that spring he had never shown any interest or desire to perform. He was reputed to be a loner, a serious student who preferred the companionship of books to friends. His shift in focus had been a matter of chance. In April, on his way home from the chemistry lab, he had walked past the open door of the auditorium where auditions were being held for the school's annual production of a Gilbert and Sullivan operetta. Tim stopped to watch.

The director needed more students for the crowd scenes. With considerably urging from his classmates, Tim, known for his distant reserve and abstracted manner, was pressured to go on stage. His natural confusion won a big round of applause, and the director gave him a song to sing, more for comic relief than for Tim's native talents.

He spent the next months rehearsing. The activity of the theatre group had tremendous appeal for Tim who, until that time, had had little to do with the social life of the school. The show was a success; Tim's small part and his vague stage presence was a hit with the audience.

This success led Tim to consider trying out for the summer theater group. Although the idea of Tim's spending two months with a theater group seemed totally out of his character, his father kept his reservations to himself. He said that it took a lot of self-control on his part to support what he felt was a waste of time, given Tim's talents. He was even less pleased when it turned out that he had to pay for Tim's room and board.

"I must have written him a dozen letters telling him to come home and get a job and drop the nonsense. If he had talent, it would have been another story. The only smart thing I did was to tear up the letters instead of sending them."

Toward the end of the summer Tim called his father and said he thought he might come home. He had had minor parts in a couple of plays, but most of the time he had sat around and found that way of life boring.

Regardless of how Tim's experience turned out, his venture into the theatrical world had been an extremely important step in Tim's development. Through his association with the theater group, Tim had acquired social self-confidence. For the first time, his father realized, Tim had made a few close friends, including a first girl friend. Furthermore, Tim could now make a real commitment to his work in science.

Psychologically healthy development during adolescence must include experiences that are failures, defeats, frustrations, or perhaps inappropriate from an adult perspective. Only through such experiences do adolescents honestly discover what they are good at and what they are not so good at, what they find challenging, enjoyable, and self-fulfilling, and what they find dull, dreary, or simply not for them.

Given a chance, adolescents go through their trials and errors without any prompting from parents or teachers. We don't have to go out of our way to encourage teenagers to try themselves out in a variety of ways or to make plenty of errors in the course of their trials. But adults can interfere with this natural process of growth, and we should avoid it. Even though all of us have lived through our own adolescent trials and certainly made our personal share of errors, we tend to forget our less successful efforts to grow up. From the perspective of adulthood, we may view our own adolescence as somewhat smoother than it actually was, and when we use our remembered experiences as the norm, adolescents today seem to be going through many more trials and making more errors. When we are successful in our discouragement of adolescents' whims, we may indeed temporarily avoid some of the errors teenagers make, but we also inhibit their psychological growth. Without taking chances now and then, without running the risks of making some mistakes, a teenager's process of growing into maturity is inevitably distorted. Parents can't realistically expect adolescence to be a time of stable, calm, and peaceful existence. Some errors, some troubles, some worries, are a healthy part of every adolescent's self-discovery, and parents must learn to accept and live with this basic fact of human growth.

One of the problems that disturbs parents most is the inconsistency of their adolescent's level of achievement. Teenagers often go through periods of little or no apparent achievement. School grades may go down; participation in extracurricular activities may suffer; it seems as if the adolescent can't do anything right. Parents come to us confused and angry, sometimes blaming their adolescent for being "lazy," sometimes blaming the school, their adolescent's friends, television, the movies, society, just about anything as the reason for the apparent drop in achievement.

At these times it may be hard for a parent to accept and understand that in the long run, for the greatest achievement, adolescents must discover their own talents, and the process of discovery is bound to involve some periods of little or no external success. If parents are aware that these times of apparently low achievement may in fact be important stages in an adolescent's self-discovery, a good deal of pressure on both parents and teenagers may be relieved. It is far better for adolescents to try themselves out in ways that sometimes lead to temporary failure than never to have the opportunity to discover what their talents are and what they are not.

From time to time parents tell us about teenagers in families other than their own who seem to breeze through everything, always appear to achieve at the highest level, and never have any difficulties. They usually hold up these apparent paragons of virtue to their children as examples of "what you could do if you really wanted to"—as if their own teenagers were deliberately not achieving in order to be spiteful to their parents. Although "failure for spite" does occasionally occur, it certainly isn't a common phenomenon, and chances are that an adolescent's lack of achievement is not motivated by a desire to hurt one's parents. In any event, using other adolescents as a whip to beat some motivation into your own teenager is without a doubt the least effective means of motivating him or her. About all it will gain is a feeling of hostility toward the supposed paragon and toward you.

Moreover, parents should recognize that no matter how smoothly life seems to be going from an outsider's point of view, no normal family escapes its share of problems in the course of adolescent development.

In addition to the obvious importance of accomplishment in terms of status and security, accomplishment for adolescents has special psychological significance. Being able to do something really well and being recognized by others for this skill has a profound effect on an adolescent's feelings of self-worth.

Even an adolescent's personality can be a kind of talent, as we discovered in the case of Michelle. When she came to camp, a sweet, docile fourteen-year-old, she couldn't "do anything." Not being able to do much other than be sweet and cooperative wasn't very satisfying to Michelle. She wanted recognition and wanted to achieve. As a defense against her lack of abilities, she occasionally made fun of her own awkwardness. Beneath her amiable facade was jealousy. Several incidents occurred. Michelle destroyed the swimming ribbons one of her cabin mates won. Another time she littered the cabin with paper and her bunk lost the "neat cabin" award for the week. It was evident that Michelle sought recognition. She wasn't selected as a captain, didn't pass swim tests, and wasn't seen by her peers as anything special.

The third week of camp we made Michelle a special camper. She was taken out of her bunk and assigned as a junior assistant with the youngest group of campers. Her jobs were to read stories at bedtime, to help the younger children get to their activities on time, and to sit with them at meal times. For the rest of the day she was encouraged to be with her own age group.

The younger children responded immediately. Michelle was their favorite counselor for the simple reason that she smiled a lot. The fact that Michelle wasn't an athlete or a performer wasn't of concern. The younger children valued her talent for smiling and her good humor. Michelle was being recognized for her prize qualities.

Within a short time Michelle requested and received special help in swimming. She had decided to assist the counselor with the group at swimming and thought she should have a swimmer's card. Next, she wrote a script for the group to perform in the weekly stunt night. Winners were determined by vote, and Michelle campaigned vigorously. Her group came in first one week.

About the middle of the season we asked Michelle if she wanted to return to her own bunk or to continue serving as a part-time assistant with the youngest group. She said she wanted to stay put until after she finished her swim tests. She was proud of all the different things she discovered herself able to do, like writing a script, making up bedtime stories. As a consequence of achieving success in handling the young campers, she had developed a sense of competence that was generalizing to other aspects of her life.

We surveyed a number of adults who were successful in their chosen vocations about particular events of their adolescence which they felt had had an impact on their future lives. For one musician a turning point had been an award for musical excellence; for a writer the memory of being editor of a high school newspaper was of special stimulus in pushing her to future success.

An early talent, however, wasn't always related to future accomplishments. One social scientist reported that he had felt inadequate as a young child; he felt that he didn't do very well in anything he tried. However, during adolescence he had had the opportunity to build a summer cabin. He hadn't had the slightest idea of how to go about it, but through trial and error he managed to put a one-room log cabin together. The cabin, he recalled, was hardly an architectural wonder. The boards were too widely spaced and a lot of caulking was necessary to fill in the gaps. The two-by-four uprights slanted. However, the building was serviceable and held up. More important than the building itself was this man's sense of having done something on his own, and equally important, he was recognized by others as a person who succeeded at a really tough job. According to this man, the sense of competence he derived from this experience began to generalize to other areas of his life, and gradually, as he became a young adult, he developed a broader sense of being a competent person. This man was fortunate. A minor talent for carpentry during adolescence was appreciated by adults, and the achievement began a cycle of accomplishment in other areas.

All too often, however, parents and teachers consider only a narrow range of conventional achievements such as school grades or athletic accomplishments as worthwhile. Parents have told us, "I know my daughter is wonderful with young children. People tell me she is the best baby-sitter they've ever had. I could do without such praise. It would be far better if she brought home a good report card once in awhile."

"I don't want to hear my son is great at raking yards. He's not going to make it in this world raking yards."

A mother told us resentfully that the school always called

her daughter when they needed a responsible student to
help out in the school office. "There's no reward for trust-
worthiness. I would like to see her spend her time achieving
the same kind of outstanding work in something to do with
school."

The valedictorians and the athletic heroes are easily identified and appreciated by family, teachers, and parents. But
parents must go beyond the conventional in appreciating
their teenagers, recognizing that life is made up of much
more than school grades or athletic performances. It is not
the talents that parents want their children to have that
count, but rather the talents their youngsters actually
possess. Fixing cars, playing a musical instrument, taking
care of younger children, getting involved in community activities—whatever an adolescent's talents might be, parents
must recognize them and be sure their adolescents know
their individual talents are truly appreciated.

*Remember that getting good grades or doing well in
athletics are by no means the only areas of meaningful
achievement for adolescents. There is certainly more to
life than high grades and sports awards. So regardless of
what your adolescent's achievements may be, pay attention to them and appreciate those particular talents.*

Guidelines for Rational Parenting

For the adolescent, identifying one's own talents must be a
process of self-discovery, not a matter of being told by someone else that you are good in one thing and not so good in
another. Nevertheless, a rational parent can serve as a
valuable sounding board in the adolescent's trial-and-error
search for his or her particular interests and abilities. Therefore, rather than telling your adolescent what direction to
pursue, be prepared to listen, to be an audience, without

trying to impose your own views.

In the course of this search, expect your adolescent to take byways that, on the surface at least, don't make much sense to you. Recognize and appreciate these temporary moves in one direction or another as an important part of the process of self-discovery, and clearly convey the message that the process of self-discovery is of crucial importance.

If your adolescent asks for your opinion, express your views honestly, directly, and without beating around the bush. But at the same time, make it clear that these are *your* views, and emphasize that what really counts is how your adolescent feels. Similarly, if your adolescent asks for factual information that you have, by all means provide the information as objectively as you can. In short, in the adolescent's search for his or her own talents, the rational parent listens more than tells, encourages rather than directs, informs but doesn't evaluate.

Your Own Values

Let your adolescent know your own values, ideas, hopes, and goals—but remember that sharing these values does not mean trying to impose them.

Applications for college were due on the first of January. In November Merle visited college campuses, collected applications, arranged for teacher recommendations, and completed the final test necessary for admission. Because she was an honor student, a participant in a wide range of activities, and had superior test scores, Merle's parents, the guidance staff, and Merle herself felt relatively confident about her acceptance. In December, after the applications were typed and ready to be mailed, Merle announced to her parents that she wasn't going to college the following year.

"What about the applications?"

"I tore them up." She ran up to her room and brought down the papers, torn into fragments.

"You can't do this to us." Her parents were distraught.

"What do you mean, I can't do this to you? Who's going to college, you or me?"

"You're a fool. Throwing away your life. What are you going to do?"

"I don't know."

"Go for a year," her father pleaded. "If it doesn't work out, okay, you can take time off."

Merle said she not only wasn't going to bow to their wishes

and try college for a year, but if they kept up the pressure, she would leave high school before graduation.

"Is that a threat?"

"It's not a threat," she retorted. "It's the way things are, take it or leave it."

"How are you going to live?"

"That's my worry."

"We're not going to give you one damn penny," her father said. He was furious.

"If I go to college, you'll support me?" she asked.

"That's it, Merle."

"Why won't you give me the money you would give me if I went?"

Her parents were astonished that Merle could be so naive as to assume they would even entertain the thought of giving her an allowance or supporting her if she didn't go on to school.

"Why?" her mother pleaded. "Why would you do such a thing? Why would you throw everything over?"

"What's everything? I don't even know what I want to do with my life. I don't know who I am."

Merle agreed to talk to us at her parent's urging. She was perfectly rational about her decision. Repeatedly she said, "I've got to find out who I am—who is Merle? All I've ever done, all I've been is what other people wanted me to be. My folks wanted a good student; I was a good student. The teachers wanted me to do the right things; I've done the right things. I've never caused trouble. Good Merle. Reliable Merle. Merle will play the piano for the school assembly. Merle will set up the chairs in the auditorium for the theater production. Merle will sing a solo in the glee club performance. Merle spends the weekend with grandparents and takes them for drives. I know what everyone in my family and school wants me to be—but me, I don't know who me is.''

Her father's reaction to Merle's search was "She's going to find out who she is without one penny from me. The trouble with her is she's had everything. When we were growing up, we didn't have the time or the freedom to worry about that Who am I? nonsense."

Her mother's reaction was depressed. Why did this have to happen to us? "There wasn't any hint of this. Merle has been a happy girl. I feel like I've been hit with a bombshell. I am so embarrassed. After all I've done for her. It doesn't make any sense to me. This kind of thing happens in other families, I never thought my daughter would do this. What is she going to do with herself? She's not trained to do anything. She has so much talent, and she's willing to throw it all away. Why can't she discover herself going to college? That's what we've always planned for her."

Her mother's final statement, "That's what we've always planned for her," is the core in this case. Merle's parents had planned and Merle had reached an age where she resented being manipulated.

When Merle's parents finally accepted the fact that their daughter needed a period of trial and error, the family could work toward a compromise. Merle had enough credits to graduate early from high school. Her father encouraged her to apply for college but to take off the last half of her senior year and the summer to do with as she wished. If she stayed at home, she wouldn't have to pay for room and board. But she would have to support herself in other respects. For example, if she traveled or looked for a job in another community, she would be expected to pay her own way. In the event that her plans didn't work out, she would have the option of attending college in the fall. Merle decided to live at home and work. After several months of employment, the reality of working without special skills or training convinced Merle that further education was necessary. In the fall going away to school was her decision, not her parents'.

The basic psychological problem of adolescence is establishing a secure sense of identity. From the adolescent's point of view this is essentially the answer to the question "Who am I?" Prior to adolescence the child's sense of self derives first from an awareness of his or her own body, and later on children begin to see themselves in terms of their roles as sons or daughters, students in school, members of a club or an athletic team.

During adolescence, however, there develops a fundamental, inner sense of self, an identity that goes beyond physical sensations or social roles. To a large extent this sense of "Who I am" depends upon what Erik Erikson has called the adolescent's ideology. This ideology is the basic framework within which adolescents look at themselves and their world, and most important, evaluate their day-to-day experiences. Essentially, these are the ideas that adolescents use to make sense of the world, plus the value system that is the basis for making judgments of right and wrong, good and bad.

Instead of thinking about one's self in terms of a variety of physical sensations or a number of different roles, the adolescent's ideology provides a basis for gaining an integrated sense of self that gives inner direction and meaning to one's life.

In the course of developing their own sense of identity, adolescents often try out a variety of points of view, sometimes swinging from one extreme to another in a very short time. For example, a teenager may go through periods of intense religious concern, become very observant of particular

religious practices, and seem utterly convinced of certain religious beliefs. Then, without any apparent reason, the
religious interests may be dropped, and that same adolescent will go through a period of active political interest,
perhaps switching from a very conservative to a radical point
of view. These changes do not stem from a lack of serious,
sincere interest on the adolescent's part. Rather, they reflect a
normal pattern of trial and error in adolescents' search for a
set of beliefs and values that will provide an ideological
framework for their own sense of identity.

Philip astonished his parents with plans to go West and
work on a ranch. They didn't feel that working on a ranch
was intrinsically wrong; however, considering the fact that
Philip was born and raised in an urban environment, the
choice didn't make much sense. His father thought that at
best Philip's wish was for a romantic escape. At worst, it
might be unsafe.

"I knew if I tried to stand in his way, we were going to run
into a problem. I told him how I felt. All I asked him was, if
he was set on going, could we check it out first."

Philip's father helped him make inquiries, and the week
school was over Philip left for the ranch. After a few weeks of
living above a stable, he wrote home telling his father he
wasn't sure whether he wanted to "stick it out" for the summer. Ranch life turned out to be somewhat different from
Philip's imaginative picture.

Part of growing up is learning what one wants to savor as
an experience and what one wants to live. Although Philip's
mother felt she could have predicted that ranch life would
be a disappointment, she recognized that the best thing she
did in terms of a long-term relationship with her son was to
share her beliefs and then let Philip discover for himself what
life was actually like. Because she did not fight his idea, he

was willing to let her share in the planning and as she stated, "At least I knew he was safe and well and that was very important to me."

Not all of a teenager's trials and errors involve extreme and dramatic shifts from one point of view to another. Sometimes we are not even aware of the changes going on in the adolescents with whom we live. Nevertheless, we must recognize that adolescence is normally a time of deep concern about what is true and false, good and bad, right and wrong. It is a period of very serious involvement with values, hopes, and ideals that will eventually become the basis for the adolescent's inner core of identity.

Most parents realize that their teenagers are going through a stage in which the beliefs and values of childhood, once accepted without question, are being reexamined and reevaluated. And sometimes parents become worried that their teenager will entirely reject the parents' values and way of life. This often leads to arguments that rapidly grow in emotional intensity and rarely resolve anything. The parent becomes convinced that the adolescent is on the road to perdition, and the adolescent usually ends up feeling misunderstood, rejected, and angry.

Undoubtedly the worst outcome of these arguments is a breakdown in communication between parents and their adolescents. Parents may feel so worried and anxious that they can't even begin talking about anything important with their adolescent without getting angry. Similarly, adolescents may feel that the situation is hopeless, that there is no way they can get their parents to understand their point of view, and they may withdraw into a shell of sullen resentment. As a result, all meaningful communication between parent and teenager is blocked, and everyone involved feels frustrated and angry.

In view of this often highly charged emotional situation, it is perhaps ironic that adolescents, during this time of their life probably more than at any other, need to share their views with others. Many adolescents do a lot of this sharing with their friends in informal, everyday conversations that give them a chance to find out what others their own age believe and feel is important. But no matter how much they share with their peers, they also need to share their feelings, their beliefs, their tentative hopes and ideals with significant adults in their lives. Equally important, they need to learn about the values, beliefs, ideals and hopes of these adults, not merely to imitate them but to discover what others who have lived through adolescence have come to believe and value. Only through this kind of mutual sharing can adolescents confidently develop their own values and achieve a secure, mature sense of identity.

By all means, share your own values, ideals, hopes and goals with your adolescent, but be sure it is a mutual exchange. Letting your adolescent know how you feel and what you believe is important, but listening and understanding the feelings and beliefs of your adolescent is equally important. Make your sharing an informal part of everyday discussions and conversation. Let it grow naturally out of your daily experiences together.

No adolescent wants to be simply a carbon copy of another person, regardless of how loved or respected that other person might be. Every psychologically healthy adolescent must experience a feeling of growing independence, a sense of being a unique individual in his or her own right. In fact, this developing independence and individuality are among the most important characteristics of an adolescent who is in the process of becoming a happy, effective, and well-integrated adult. Therefore, while it is extremely important that you let your adolescent know about your own values, your ideals, hopes, and goals, they must be honestly *shared,* not *imposed.*

Listen with respect for your adolescent's growing independence and unique individuality. Don't give lectures; don't try to impose your views; and don't fight about who is right and who is wrong, who is good and who is bad. You and your adolescent can, and undoubtedly will, differ from time to time. Remember that these differences are important for your adolescent's sense of individuality. Learn to prize these differences as a sign of your adolescent's developing independence and maturity.

Part of the problem parents encounter stems from the apparent changeability of their adolescent. Parents like to think of themselves as rational when they reach an age at which they are parenting teenagers. They plan career changes, think out shifts in residences, carefully consider investments. Changes in their own behavior, they like to think, are not whimsical and rarely occur overnight. It's annoying, worrisome, and confusing to have an adolescent who doesn't settle down easily into a mold, who isn't ready to accept one career line and follow through, who changes everything from style of dress to hairstyles with what appears to be alarming frequency. "If only my daughter would make up her mind what she wants to be," said one mother, "I'd be happy. I'd give her support."

Although few parents would like to admit it, they are eager for their children to make decisions about their futures partly because the parents are reaching an age when they would welcome a little less responsibility. As one father told us, "I hope my son doesn't get it into his head that I'm going to support him the rest of his life."

Parents today groan about how adolescents waste time trying to find themselves. Repeatedly we hear comments like "When I was young, we didn't spend this time worrying about what we were going to do and who we were." In one sense this is partly true. Parents today, at least those with children of adolescent age, did face another world. Service in the armed forces took chunks of time from the lives of many men. There was a sense of urgency in making career choices. Women had fewer opportunities, and marriage was a major goal. For adolescents today, the social climate is different. Options are greater for women. Present times encourage both boys and girls to discover themselves.

When the father of a seventeen-year-old male started pressuring his son to make a decision and stick to it, the boy retorted that he wasn't going to jump into a career like his father, stick at one job until he was in his forties, and complain every day about how he hated what he was doing.

A teenage girl who resented her parents' pressure to decide what to do with her life told us, "I've got time. Why do I have to rush?" She wanted to be sure of herself and her goals.

We aren't implying that today's adolescents are more changeable than adolescents were in the past. This is not the case. However, opportunities for trying out different roles are more widely available to adolescents now than in previous generations. One father we talked to commented on this. "When I was a teenager, I never thought in terms of choices. I went directly from high school into the army. After serving for four years, I started working and have worked in the same line of business ever since. That's the trouble with teenagers today," he added, "too much easy money without real work in one career." He believed that the problems adolescents struggle with would be solved if they went right to work and remained in the same job. Not surprisingly, his son held a different view. He couldn't see what was so great about his father starting work right after the army and staying in the same kind of business his whole life. The son felt that there had to be more to life than a job. He also felt that even though his father had had outward stability, he harbored a great deal of resentment. The son reported that on countless occasions he had heard his father expressing a wish to "throw over his whole business and walk out." He added that his father was always saying how "sick and tired" he was of routines, and the only reason he hadn't become an artist was because he had to support a family.

Expect adolescence to be a time of changes, a time of experimentation, of trying out new points of view, new interests and activities. Don't forget that this pattern of exploration and changeability is an important part of normal adolescent development and provides a foundation for a secure adult identity.

Another aspect of the problem parents face comes from their awareness that forces outside of the immediate family may have an enormous impact on their adolescent's views, and parents are concerned that these influences will be harmful. This may be a very real problem that parents must somehow deal with. Adolescents are indeed exposed to a wide variety of influences outside of the family—from peers, mass media, other adults, and institutions—and sometimes these influences are damaging. In a later chapter, Psychological Immunization, we will consider this general problem more fully. At this point we can only stress that parents *must* rely to a large extent on early family experiences to provide the adolescent with enough personal strength to guard against these potentially negative influences. We don't mean to minimize the possible dangers that an adolescent might face, but in our experience with a large number of families that have met this issue, we have found that the basic problem is much more often caused inadvertently by parental overconcern and overinvolvement than by the attraction of potentially dangerous influences outside the family.

Martha's first boyfriend at sixteen threw her parents into a panic. "With all the available boys in her class, boys who have asked her out but she refused, she accepted a date with the worst—the last kind of boy I can see my daughter dating." Her mother was dismayed at Martha's choice—a boy who came from a totally different background, had none of their values, and whose reputation in the community was questionable.

Both parents were embarrassed by the relationship and frantically concerned about their daughter's welfare. From the moment Martha accepted the first date, the family argued. Martha's mother cried and told her daughter the extent of her fears. She pictured her as having a dismal future which included pregnancy, forced marriage, leaving school, a welfare existence, divorced—in short, a ruined life. Her father equally vocally predicted one string of disasters after another. "You are making a fool of yourself. You're throwing away your life at sixteen. You play with fire and you'll get burned." He warned her that if she persisted in going out with "that boy," she would be on her own a lot quicker than she realized.

Martha's choice of boys made no sense to the family. They could not conceive of having a daughter willing to overturn her own values and values of the family all for a "mad fling."

When we talked to the parents about their need to present rationally their side to Martha instead of assulting her

with an emotional outburst, they became angry and irritated. They felt they shouldn't have to justify themselves to
a sixteen-year-old. Why did they have to play being cool and
collected? "We have seen what happens to kids when they
get caught up in these kinds of relationships," said her
mother. They completely resented the "nonsense" of psychologically talking as equals to a daughter who was little
more than a child. "We aren't her peers, we're her parents.
We damn well are going to let her know our feelings. We
will not tiptoe around her. She will get hurt. We will get
hurt. If she keeps going out with him, we're through with
her."

Talking to us about their worries, anger, and resentment
helped Martha's parents deal more rationally with the problem when they later talked to Martha.

The chance to let off steam to someone other than Martha was most important for the eventual successful outcome of this situation. When the parents did talk to
Martha, instead of presenting all the awful things they
had imagined, they restrained themselves, limiting their
reactions and comments about the young boy to some
concrete characteristics which, they told Martha, they perceived in him.

Sixteen-year-olds want parental approval. They want their
parents to like their friends. However, in spite of these in-
clinations, Martha went out with the young boy on several
dates. After the second date she told her mother she had
enough of the boy. "He's not my type." The qualities her
parents had disapproved of also bothered Martha. Their
calm presentation of "facts" had alerted their daughter to
the potential dangers. She needed to come to this decision
herself. By not discussing the subject until they cooled off,
Martha's parents had avoided creating a major blow-up.

Parents' extreme reactions can sometimes make an issue a major disaster. In this instance, low-keyed behavior on the part of Martha's parents prevented a rift in the family.

Staying loose and cool when one's adolescent flirts with potential dangers is a challenge. As parents we may feel hostility at being forced into a position of rational control when inside we may be boiling with resentment and quivering with concern. A superficial interest on the part of an adolescent can become a whole lifetime in the eyes of parents. We may resent letting youngsters get what we feel is an upper hand. We should be the ones leading. What right do they have at fifteen or sixteen to lead us?

This is precisely the time when we need to stop for a moment and ask ourselves if our whole lifetime up to that point has been blameless, faultless, conforming, without ever a gamble with the forbidden. Shifting perspectives when the going gets particularly rough or touches on very sensitive areas can create a totally different atmosphere. To express disapproval, to inject our personal reactions is a parental right, but it is often the parents' strong emotional reactions to their adolescents' initially superficial interests that lead to a counterreaction, with the adolescents becoming much more committed to a position opposing their parents primarily to defend their own integrity as individuals.

"Open frank discussion," one mother fairly shouted at us, "when I discover my son upstairs in his bedroom with a girl, the door locked?"

Another father laughed scornfully. "You must be kidding," he told us, "that I'll stand for my daughter having sex in my house and expect me to stay calm while I tell her no. She damn well will be out on her ear."

The emotional intensity of these parents' reactions makes dealing with their adolescents' sexual motivations and behaviors even more difficult than it might otherwise be. Very often, it is the parents' emotions, rather than the underlying values, that provoke the adolescent to take a rebellious stand.

Nevertheless, we certainly sympathize with and understand the parents' point of view. Frankly, on the basis of our professional experiences, we believe that the great majority of adolescents are unable to deal with the psychological consequences of sexual intercourse. Most adolescents have not yet established firmly their own sense of themselves, and the psychological intimacy of an intense sexual relationship may very well be too stressful for them to integrate comfortably and happily in their daily lives. As a result, at least in American society today, sexual experiences too early in life may indeed hamper an adolescent's social and psychological development.

Our own opinion about adolescents' use of drugs (including alcohol) is even stronger. In the course of our professional careers, we have worked with far too many adolescents whose psychological development has been seriously disrupted by the use of drugs. We are therefore unequivocally against their use.

But we must stress that these represent our own *personal* views, and by sharing them we are not trying to convince others that these opinions are necessarily or absolutely right for every parent and every adolescent. Rather, we strongly urge parents to think through these issues for themselves. We urge them to consider their own life experiences and their own values in order to establish a rational basis for their points of view. If parents can clarify and establish their own understanding of what they believe is right and wrong, and also be clear about the reasons for their beliefs, they are much less likely to overreact emotionally when they confront these issues with their teenagers. Parents will then be better prepared to express their views openly, honestly, and firmly, without getting caught up in emotionally-charged battles that get in the way of rational parenting.

One adolescent girl, sixteen years of age, said that she remembers the day her father discovered she had smoked pot. "My father smokes cigarettes. He chain smokes. I don't even smoke. I tried pot. I told him. He said if I did it again he would kill me." She told us she remembers at the time being shaken by her father's explosive words. All she could imagine were newspaper headlines. "Father stabs daughter who smoked pot."

In current life it seems that three topics—sex, drugs, and alcohol—top the list of taboos adolescents and parents have trouble in freely discussing. When these subjects arise many parents become incensed and get caught up with blanket no's, warnings, threats, and other emotion-laden reactions. We encourage little children to ask "Why?" Such dialectics operating in a family are stimulating to children, and thus we grope for answers. "Why does the moon come out at night?" Fine, we can handle that question. "Why do we have to pay for candy in a store?" We can respond to these questions regarding morals and values. Suddenly at adolescence parents face a whole group of Why's which not only can't be dismissed but which the adolescent challenges. "What's so wrong with sex?" asked one adolescent. "My parents aren't so innocent." Questions such as this demand more than simple No's. Parents can hardly say, as they might to a young child, "We don't do that sort of thing." We're faced with highly charged, very personal questions, and parents' emotional outbursts are rarely helpful to the adolescent facing real and very significant choices in life.

Be careful about your own emotional overreactions that

may provoke a counterreaction, forcing your adolescent
to take a position that may in the long run be hurtful to
both of you. Think through your own views before-
hand, and be prepared to express your views openly
and firmly, but without engaging in emotional battle.

A subtle but nevertheless serious problem stems from parents' desire to have their children fulfill their own hopes and
goals. Sometimes parents are not aware of this in themselves,
but it occurs much more often than one might expect. Most of
us have had certain dreams and early ambitions at least partly,
or even entirely, frustrated. Perhaps our dreams were too
unrealistic, or the circumstances of our lives may have
prevented us from achieving these goals, but whatever the
reason, few of us completely fulfill the hopes and ambitions of
our own adolescence. And then, when we have our children,
there is a very strong temptation to transfer our own frustrated
goals and ambitions onto our children, hoping to fulfill
ourselves through the achievements of our sons or daughters.
We are frequently not even aware of what we are doing, but in
one way or another we manage to create powerful forces
pushing our adolescents in directions we wish we had taken
ourselves. And, of course, in most cases the adolescents rebel.

Joseph was destined to take over the family business.
After two daughters, his father was ecstatic about the birth
of a son. For three generations, each of a succession of sons
had stepped into the business, and the business had grown
and flourished over the years.

Joseph's training for the business began early. As a youngster, Joseph was taken down to the office simply to get used
to the surroundings and spend time with his father and
grandfather while they were at work. Later on, he was given
minor tasks to do, and gradually he took on more and more
responsibility.

Involvement in the business continued, of course, while Joseph was in high school. Other boys took part-time jobs in the community, but Joseph didn't have to look for work. It was assumed that he would work for his father and grandfather. At first acquiescent, Joseph conformed to the family pattern. From time to time he griped a bit, but the griping didn't seem to be serious. The work was not unpleasant, and he certainly made a lot more money working in the family business than he would in another job.

But when Joseph entered his senior year in high school, he refused to go back to work in the business. The family was shocked. Joseph's father couldn't understand his son's reaction. There was a very successful business to inherit. Joseph could take over the firm as soon as he was old enough, and he would not have to face the struggles for financial security that so many others encountered.

"I can't understand it," said Joseph's father. "It's something I've dreamed of ever since Joseph was born."

Joseph refused to change his mind. When he talked to us about the problem he said, "It isn't for me. It's not the life I want. I worked for Dad because he expected me to. I knew what it meant to him. I didn't want to hurt him. My dad's a great guy in a lot of ways. It's only that he has it in his head that the business will be turned over to me."

Joseph's father had a great deal of difficulty understanding Joseph's "changed" feelings. "He's never told me what he felt. He enjoyed himself. I can't believe he hated everything about the company."

Joseph said it wasn't all hate. Rather he had learned to dull his feelings, keep them in check. Now that he was growing older, he wanted to do what he wanted the rest of his life. The money had been a lure. However, he was set on going into science.

Joseph made the break. After high school he entered a university, majoring in science. It has taken his father considerable time to get over what he first perceived as a rejection, and he has only recently tried to understand that Joseph had to go his own way—follow his own talents and desires for a career.

Adolescents don't necessarily want to fulfill their parents' dreams and ambitions; they rightfully want to lead their own lives, build their own hopes, and achieve their own goals. Parents might rationalize their "pushiness" by arguing that they only want what is best for their children, implying that they (the parents) know what is best for their adolescents. But when we really face ourselves as parents and as human beings, by and large we recognize this argument as largely a rationalization that can do little good either for ourselves or for our adolescents. Parental concern, interest, involvement, and sharing are obviously important in every adolescent's life; but equally important is parental respect for the adolescent's independence and individuality.

Be especially careful about the temptation to transfer your own goals and ambitions onto your adolescent, hoping perhaps to fulfill your frustrated dreams through your child's life. Whenever you find yourself in conflict with your adolescent's views and you start saying, "I know what is best for you," check out your own hopes and dreams, and be sure that you are really concerned with what is best for your adolescent rather than with your own desires.

Guidelines for Rational Parenting

In discussing your own values, goals, hopes, and ideals with your adolescent, remember that adolescents are usually in the process of developing their own sense of values.

Therefore, they are likely to be somewhat unsure of themselves, even though this may be covered up by a blustering, overly confident manner, and a highly critical view of other people's opinions. In most instances, this bluster and critical hostility is a defensive reaction stemming from the fact that the adolescent has not yet established a secure sense of confidence in his or her own point of view.

To minimize your adolescent's defensiveness in these conversations, rational parents take a stance of equality rather than superiority, they are open-minded rather than dogmatic, and they share their views rather than try to convince the adolescent that parental opinions are best.

Equal rather than superior. There is nothing more likely to elicit an adolescent's defensiveness than an adult who seems to be "looking down his nose" at the adolescent. Thus, when you discuss your own values, remember that both of you have equal rights to your respective points of view. Regardless of how firmly convinced you are of your own point of view, make sure you avoid any suggestion, either direct or indirect, of superiority.

Open-minded rather than dogmatic. Think about how you react to someone who is so dogmatic that he or she can see only one point of view—his or her own—as legitimate. Trying to talk with this kind of person is usually a frustrating, irritating experience. For an adolescent talking with an adult, especially a parent, this kind of dogmatism only leads to greater defensivenss and blocks mutual understanding. So be careful about being dogmatic, not only in what you say but also in how you say it. Express your own views as forcefully and as strongly as you feel them, but be clear that these are *your* views and that you are fully aware that your views are not the only ones that are legitimate.

Sharing, not imposing. The goal of your discussion with your adolescent is to gain greater mutual understanding, not to convince your adolescent that your views are the only right ones. Of course, the rational parent believes strongly in his or her views. But even more fundamentally, rational parents respect their adolescent's right to develop his or her own values.

Response To Crisis

*When a crisis occurs, your job as a parent is to
provide immediate, unconditional support—
and for the time being, at least,
to forget about trying to reform or
remodel your adolescent.*

Crises are inevitable in adolescence. They seem to be an intrinsic part of every teenager's life. One parent commented, "I feel like I'm living on the brink of disaster. I never know what's going to happen next. I tell you if he comes home once more with a problem, I'm packing my suitcases and leaving. I'll be the one running away."

Adults have their own problems and they have already experienced their own share of adolescent traumas, so having to live through another round of adolescent crises often seems to be one of the more unreasonable demands of adult life. Nevertheless, dealing with the crises of adolescent life is unavoidable.

Recognize and accept the fact that some crises are normal and to be expected in every adolescent's life.

The problems that generate crises are usually difficult enough for the teenager to deal with, but in some instances they are complicated even further by a parent's emotional reactions. Sometimes relatively minor problems are made more serious by a parent's reactions, and without either parents or adolescent being quite aware of how things seem suddenly to grow out of proportion, a trivial issue becomes a major crisis. This is what happened to Lisa during her senior year in high school.

Since her freshman year, Lisa had been a member of the school's theatrical group. She had served an apprenticeship hauling scenery, painting sets, typing scripts, and acting in a number of the productions. At the start of her last year she auditioned for the senior play. Because seniors traditionally were awarded principal roles, she felt fairly confident about getting the part she wanted.

The cast was announced. Lisa was given a minor role. To make matters worse, the girl who got the part that Lisa felt she deserved was a sophomore. Lisa's mother shared her disappointment. She agreed with Lisa that the director was at fault. It was a clear instance of favoritism. She told Lisa, "If I were you, I would have nothing to do with those people. They used you, took advantage. You have no business wasting your time."

"No one worked harder than my daughter," Lisa's mother told us. "The unfairness is what hurts. She deserved the chance to be a star in her senior year after all the time she put into the theater."

At her mother's suggestion Lisa dropped out of the play. Her senior year was not particularly happy. She missed the excitement of being involved with a group of her friends and the theater.

The initial problem was not very serious. Without the mother's subsequent emotional reactions it would probably have resolved itself without much difficulty, as it did with one of Lisa's friends who was also slighted in the cast selection. Diane, also a senior, was given a minor role. However, in contrast to Lisa, Diane was encouraged to continue.

Diane's mother said she, too, had been resentful about

the teacher. She had considered talking to the principal and making an issue of the unfairness. "Diane cried for days, she was so unhappy."

However, instead of going to the principal or the director, she told Diane, "You're right in the way you feel, but you want to be in the play. You're going to make your part a hit. You'll have the fun. You'll be the winner in the long run."

With her mother's support, Diane worked on her part and made the minor role a "sensation." Diane's senior year ended on a high note when the school review of the show cited her performance as outstanding.

In Lisa's case, the fact that her mother took the anger about the crisis one step further resulted in a major trauma. Lisa ended up telling her mother, "If it hadn't been for you, I probably would have done what Diane did; I could have had a good time like her."

In this instance, as in many other similar situations, we suspect that the mother's strong emotional reactions resulted not only from her concern about her daughter but also from her own feelings of being slighted. In any event, a bit more parental restraint would undoubtedly have helped Lisa have a much more satisfying year in high school.

When a crisis occurs, control your emotional reactions, particularly your anger; if you do get angry and have to express your anger, do it when your adolescent isn't around. Some healthy displacement of your anger, directed at some cheap dishes, a solid wall, or any other safe, inanimate object, can be most useful at these times.

Sometimes parents' emotional reactions lead them to *overgeneralize* about their adolescent, and those overgeneralizations add further fuel to the emotional fire set off by the crisis. One of our sons took the family car for a Saturday night date. The next morning he slept late. We had to use the car, and when we went outside, we discovered a scratch and a small dent on one of the fenders. When did this happen? We studied the dent and the scratch, trying to remember if either one of us had damaged the car. There was no question in our minds that it had happened the previous evening. We hauled the youngster out of bed.

"Why didn't you tell us about the accident?"

"What accident?" Still half asleep, he denied having been in an accident.

"Did you see the car? Go out and take a look at the fender."

He did as he was told.

"Did you see it?"

"Yes."

"A new car. . . ."

"It's six months old," he interrupted defensively.

"That's a new car as far as we're concerned. You get the chance to use a new car, and you bring it back a *wreck.*"

"It's not a wreck. I can hardly see the scratch."

"Hardly see the scratch!" we exploded. We took him outside with us and pointed to the dent.

"How did it happen?"

"I don't know."

"What do you mean you don't know? You get in an accident, and you tell us you don't know you were in an accident."

"I wasn't in an accident," he argued.

"So the car got banged up just sitting all by itself."

"No."

"Then something happened."

"I was parked."

"Where were you parked?"

"Near a building."

"You drove past a building and scratched the car?"

We had him on the defensive. The garbled story finally came out that he had been parked behind the gym at his school. As he drove out of the lot, he cut too close to the edge of the building and scratched the car.

"Didn't you hear what was happening?"

"Yes, I heard something."

"Then why didn't you stop? Why did you keep on driving?"

"I had to go forward. If I had gone backwards it would have been worse. Last night I looked at it. It didn't look bad. I thought it was dirt."

"You thought it was dirt! You shouldn't have cut close to the building. It was careless. You weren't thinking. That's the trouble. You weren't thinking. We've told you a car isn't a toy. You don't deserve to drive a good car."

And then, while our youngster was obviously beginning to feel utterly miserable, we stepped up the attack. That's how he treated his possessions. We reminded him of the time he left the lawn mower out in the rain. We had told him to bring the lawn mower in because it was going to rain. He had insisted it wasn't going to rain, and he would bring it in later. He was wrong. A cloudburst came within the hour.

We brought up the time he had taken all his toy trucks to the park even though we told him not to take his trucks with him, or if he did, to be sure to bring them home. He forgot. By the time we went back, the trucks were gone. We reminded him of the time he left the phonograph on. How many times had we told him to make sure his stereo set was turned off? We managed to drag up a long series of incidents stretching back sixteen years that demonstrated his lack of respect for property. We really had him this time, guilty without doubt, and we prosecuted him for all (and even a good deal more than) it was worth.

"Okay," he told us bitterly, "I'll never drive again." He threw down the car keys and stormed out of the room. Clearly, we had "won" our case.

But when we had calmed down and gained some perspective on what we had been saying, we realized that our overgeneralizations were obviously irrational. The toy truck episode had occurred when he was four years old. In countless aspects, our son was a fine person, sensitive to the feelings of others, intelligent, and from an ethical point of view mature and responsible. The incident of the previous night did reflect poor judgment. But then how many times in our driving careers had we scraped tires against curbs when we misjudged distances? How many times had we managed to put in some small dents and then never talked about them? We learned later that he had been in a hurry because the girl whom he had taken to a school play had to be home by 11 p.m. When the play ended at eleven, she had been anxious about the time, and he had become tense about his driving.

In any event, the damage to the car was trivial, and our emotional reaction was entirely out of proportion to the reality of the situation. In the heat of the moment we dredged up incidents from the past that were entirely irrelevant, overgeneralizing to make our case even stronger. We played the role of prosecutor, and nearly managed to make a crisis out of a very unimportant incident. Fortunately, even we were shocked by some of our more melodramatic statements, and we stopped the prosecution before it got out of hand. The experience didn't do our son much good, but at least it sensitized us to the danger all parents feel from their own emotional reactions.

Be careful about overgeneralizing at times of great stress. Stick to the immediate problem, and stop worrying about potential long-range dangers.

Periods of crisis are clearly *not* appropriate times for moral instruction. When adolescents are suffering the pangs of some trauma, regardless of whether or not the trauma is a result of their own behavior, it is unreasonable to expect them to respond positively to parental statements of "I told you so" or to lessons about prudence and morality.

At 12 p.m. on a Saturday night, friends of ours were called by the local police. Their son, John, along with a group of six other boys, had been taken into custody. The parents of each of the boys were being called. Stunned, the parents drove to the police station. The officer on duty said that the boys had been caught vandalizing street signs in the community, causing disturbances to pedestrians, and they faced possible charges.

It was a first offense for the group. All were local youngsters known to the police through their involvement in athletic groups. Because of their age, as well as the fact that the people who had been bothered were reluctant to press charges, the boys were released in the custody of their parents.

"We've warned him time and again," John's parents told the police officer, "if he ran around with that crowd, he would get into trouble. He wouldn't listen. He had all the answers. He thought he knew what was right. We've begged him. We've done eveything we could, but he was stubborn. Now we'll see what happens. We'll see where this gets him."

We saw John and his parents the following morning. They continued their tirade against him. They had seen it coming. They could have predicted this would occur. If it hadn't been the police, it would have been something else.

Throughout the tirade John remained sullenly silent, but he finally broke down and tried to answer his parents. He said that they made fun of all his friends. The boys hadn't been doing what the police said. It was all a mistake. He accused his parents of never having warned him about that crowd of boys.

"We didn't tell you!" exclaimed his father. "What do you think we were saying?"

"Nothing."

One accusation after another occurred. The parents recounted all the good, sound moral advice they had been giving their son over the past months. One moment John denied they had said anything, and in the next breath he contradicted himself and said they never approved of anything he did.

At this point John was vulnerable. He had been warned by the police. An evening with his friends that began innocently enough got out of hand. Plunging into morality lectures, reminding him of their predictions of such occurrences was certainly not going to have any beneficial effect on John's future behavior. At this time the parents' condemnation only aggravated the original problem. John was miserably uncomfortable, feeling trapped and helpless, and no amount of "I told you so's" could be helpful in the least.

Don't use periods of crisis for purposes of moral instruction or as opportunities to force changes in behavior that you think are desirable. Remember that instruction at these times rarely has any positive effect and may very likely have unexpected and undesirable consequences.

It certainly isn't easy for parents to control their emotional reactions when their fifteen-year-old daughter tells them she thinks she is pregnant, when they discover their adolescent might be using drugs, when their teenager comes home obviously drunk. These are not trivial issues, and parents must face them and deal with them. Parents cannot and should not behave like nonemotional robots, but some degree of self-control can reasonably be expected. If you feel that you must explode when a crisis erupts, by all means do so—but go off on your own, as far away from your adolescent as you can get, and swear as much as you like, beat the walls if you must, even throw a few dishes if that makes you feel better. We mean this quite seriously; some opportunity to let off steam can be very useful in a crisis, as long as the steam isn't directed at the adolescent. The last thing teenagers need when they are facing an important problem and trying to deal with their own emotions is the emotional reactions of their parents.

The prime responsibility of parents when their teenagers meet a crisis is to provide immediate and unconditional support. More than at any other time in their lives, when adolescents are in a crisis, they need to feel totally accepted and sustained by their parents, regardless of what has gone on before and without any conditions attached. Don't attach conditions to your parental support—"if you promise to be good" or "if you change" or "if you will listen to me." All of these "ifs" establish conditions for parental support and to a large extent weaken the effectiveness of the parent's response. Deal with issues of possible change later on, after the shock of the crisis has passed. Parents sometimes feel that their teenagers are most vulnerable at a time of crisis, and indeed they are, and parents may jump at this opportunity to force their teenagers to change their behavior. But changes achieved in this way are almost always temporary. Even more important, this kind of parental reaction leaves teenagers feeling that they have been taken advantage of and perhaps even cheated right at the time they need their parents' support without any conditions attached.

A turning point in Eleanor and her father's relationship came as a result of his unqualified support at a critical moment. After a family argument, she had taken his car, packed a suitcase, and left home. Several hours after departing she was on the phone. She had smashed the car but wasn't hurt.

"What do I do?"

The father recalled that his first reaction to this "last straw" in her rebellious behavior was to tell her off. Instead, he drove a hundred miles in the middle of the night to where she was stranded. As he put it, the several hours gave him a chance to cool down.

Arriving at the scene of the accident, he took charge, arranging for the car to be towed and talking to the police. On the trip home he made a point of discussing every subject he could think of other than the accident. Later he sat down with her while they both ate breakfast.

"I didn't even ask her to make coffee. I served her. I knew she expected me to explode. It was probably lucky I was tired out with the driving."

He let her talk—a long rambling story about how she felt. He listened. Nothing more was said about the incident for the next several days. When Eleanor seemed less tense, her father brought up the subject. He talked about Eleanor's responsibility to help pay for the car's repair and how he felt about her running away. She, in turn, accepted her responsibility and reacted more maturely than ever before. We spoke to her several months later about the incident, and it was clear that for her the most important aspect of the entire experience was her father's unconditional support at a time of crisis. She felt that he treated her as an adult, and as a result, she began to behave as an adult.

Providing adolescents with support is not necessarily easy, even when parents control their emotional reactions and inhibit their tendency to "teach a lesson." When adolescents confront a crisis, they are likely to be very touchy, ready to explode or withdraw, and parents may not be aware of the cause. Adolescents are caught in a dilemma: on the one hand, they are striving to be independent from their parents, and on the other, they need to depend on people they can trust. Thus, when problems occur, they are in a conflict between the need to be independent and the need to be dependent, a conflict that is intensified by their own emotional reactions to their problems. As a result, their behavior is most likely to be inconsistent, swinging from one extreme of wanting to solve their problem strictly on their own to the other extreme of demanding help, support, and nurturance. Accompanying these swings in behavior is often an extremely heightened sensitivity to any real or imagined slight on the part of their parents.

This interpretation of an adolescent's response to periods of crisis is not intended to excuse the adolescent's behavior, but the important issue is not excuse or blame. Rather, it is a matter of understanding, for if parents can understand the adolescent's dilemma, there is a greater chance that they will be able to exercise the self-control and patience that is required during their youngster's moments of stress.

Parental support is a very general term that covers a wide range of behaviors. The most important support you can give is your undivided attention. With all the other demands on time and energy, providing this individual attention may not be easy, but at a time when your teenager is undergoing a great deal of stress, there are probably few other things you can do that are as important in the long run as paying attention to your troubled child.

The actual time demanded may not be very lengthy, as Patricia's parents discovered, but that time was crucial and well worth whatever else they had to give up. Patricia wasn't invited to the Junior dance. Her friends were going, and as is typical with these events, the planning went on weeks ahead of the evening. Patricia's parents could not help her. When they tried to explain that she would have lots of social dates later on in life, she turned on them in anger, "You don't understand how I feel."

"Of course I know how she felt," said Patricia's mother. "One look at that long face was enough. The dance was on her mind constantly. There was nothing I could do. I thought of asking one of her cousins to take her, but she screamed at me when I hinted at that solution."

On the evening of the dance Patricia became extremely withdrawn. She went to her room and turned on her record player. Her parents were getting ready to go out to dinner—a long-standing engagement with friends. Patricia's mother recalled standing outside her daughter's door, listening to the music. She was just about to tell Patricia they were leaving when she decided instead to tell her husband they should stay home.

"I changed clothes. Patricia came into the bedroom and asked me why I had changed. I didn't lie to her. All I said was we didn't feel like going. She went back to her room. Later that evening she came down to the kitchen, and we sat around the table talking. We must have talked until three that morning—about everything. No one mentioned the school dance. It's been a long time since she kissed us good-night. That evening we got hugs and kisses. Any other time I never would have dreamed of staying home. It was worth it for her sake that night."

During the crucial period of stress, give your adolescent individual attention, and remember that a small dose of undivided attention at the right time can have enormously important psychological effects.

In addition to time and undivided attention, providing parental support also means trying to empathically understand what your adolescent is experiencing at the moment, without making judgments, without analyzing motives, without trying to figure out some neat and comfortable solution that will satisfy you. Your goal is to share empathically your teenager's feelings—the self-doubts, the confusion, anger, depression, guilt, whatever these feelings might be, and to listen sympathetically without trying to instruct, to correct, to change.

The core of parental support at the moment of a crisis should be empathic, nonjudgmental sharing and sympathetic listening. The school's guidance counselor telephoned Alan's father. His son faced expulsion from school. The father's first reaction was to "let his son sweat it out" while he continued with his business conferences. "Kids need to be taught a lesson once in a while for their own good."

Alan got on the phone. His father started to press for an explanation of what was going on and told Alan he'd be over in a couple of hours.

"I was going to hold to that when he said 'Can't you come now, Dad?' I heard a crack in that voice and decided to go over."

For the rest of the afternoon Alan talked, and his father listened. "The kid's hands were shaking. Something about the scene hit me. I remembered a scrape of my own at about the same age. I had never told Alan that story. I told him then, and I think more than anything else it helped him to know that he hadn't blown his life. He'd survive. I did—he would, too. A number of times when we talked about what he was going to do, he'd say out of the blue how he never thought I was going to come right away. He had expected to wait all afternoon in the school office.''

At a time of crisis, having someone back you up, serve as a support while you're trying to muddle through the emotions of the problem can make all the difference in how you cope. This is true for teenagers as well as it is for adults. In the midst of a crisis you may not see any positive consequences of the stress you and your adolescent are undergoing. Yet, we have repeatedly found that it is precisely these times of crisis which may provoke very significant psychological growth in the adolescent and immeasurably strengthen the relationship between parents and teenagers.

Guidelines for Rational Parenting
When a crisis occurs with your adolescent, keep in mind some "Dos" and "Don'ts" of rational parenting:
- Do give your adolescent undivided attention.
- Don't overreact to the problem.
- Do stay focused on the immediate problem at hand.
- Don't generalize to other situations or other times.
- Do provide as much psychological support as you can without attaching any conditions to that support.
- Don't multiply the stress by adding your own anger to the problems your adolescent must face.
- Do strive to understand how your adolescent is feeling, and convey to your adolescent your sense of empathic understanding.
- Don't moralize.

Accentuate the Positive

Remember that if you want to influence an adolescent, praise and reward are much more powerful, effective, and longer lasting than criticism and punishment.

Psychologists have tested the relative effectiveness of reward and punishment in dozens of different kinds of situations, and the results of all of these tests tell the same consistent story: In the long run, reward works much better than punishment. For parents of adolescents, this has very profound implications, for it means that many parents will want to modify their parenting style in order to positively influence their teenagers.

Frankly, most of us don't use praise nearly enough in our everyday lives. Particularly in our relationships with our children, we tend to be much more sensitive to what they are doing *wrong* than to what they are doing *right*. Thus, we are much quicker to criticize than to praise.

Teachers operate in much the same way. Recognition in school is typically reserved for outstanding students. The majority of youngsters spend four years in high school without much attention—period. Behavorial problems and academic deficiencies attract notice, and the adolescents in these instances receive attention in one form or another, but certainly not praise or rewards.

We ran the following experiment in a school where students below standard in English were routinely assigned to remedial classes. Considerable stigma was attached to these special groups. The rest of the student body and the staff were very much aware that this group of youngsters had a history of failures.

We took one of these special classes and told them that at the end of the year their best writing, regardless of length, would be published in a class magazine. Every student would be represented. The one inflexible criteria was that the paragraph, theme, or sample of writing would reflect their best effort.

When word of the plan circulated in the school, there was considerable reaction. A magazine for honors' classes was all right, but publishing writing of remedial students was considered an outrage. The opposition didn't deter us. During the next months each pupil worked on writing skills. Their teacher repeatedly returned compositions for corrections. Not one pupil objected. They were consistently reminded that if their work was to be in print with their names as bylines, they had an obligation to themselves to make certain the writing was perfect.

At the end of the year a mimeographed magazine entitled "The Best" was circulated among staff and students in the school. The reactions were mixed. The remedial students were delighted. No book or magazine was read with such thoroughness. The English honors sections compared their own compositions with the magazine's contents, finding the only difference to be that their own publication contained more poetry.

A number of the English teachers, however, expressed resentment. The chairman commented that to reward a remedial group with its own magazine might detract from the honors' publication. The fact that the students in the remedial class had achieved, been rewarded for their efforts, and that the *majority* had acquired sufficient language skills to be transferred back to regular classes was overlooked.

Be generous in your praise. Don't reserve your praise just for major achievements; whenever your adolescent does something praiseworthy, no matter how trivial it may seem at the moment, be sure to express your appreciation and your admiration.

When you see something good, something desirable, no matter how small or trivial it might be, seize the opportunity to express your honest praise. We emphasize the importance of *honest* praise. Insincere praise is worse than no praise at all, so don't fake it. You don't have to go overboard and artificially gush over some trivial thing your adolescent has done. The gushing will probably embarrass your teenager more than anything else, and sooner or later your adolescent will realize that your positive evaluations can't be trusted. But a simple, honest, straightforward word of praise can have tremendous effects.

As a parent, you can't praise your teenager too often. But if it is false praise, the trust in the relationship between parent and child is inevitably damaged. So be generous in your praise, but always be sure to be honest and sincere.

We asked a group of adolescents to write down all the things their parents had found wrong with them in the past week. The list of critical reactions was lengthy. Not keeping rooms clean; playing music too loudly; eating with poor table manners; not being clean; leaving wet towels on the bathroom floor; not using acne medicine; not watching a diet; spending too much money; not studying enough; popping gum; leaving dishes on the sink instead of putting them in a dishwasher; forgetting to walk the dog; smoking; monopolizing the telephone; baiting a sibling; tracking mud; wearing hiking boots inside the house on polished floors; bringing friends home whom the parent disapproved of; staying up too late and not being able to get up in the morning.

On the following day we asked the same group to write down any compliments or praise their parents had given in the previous week. Many of the group had trouble responding. Several boys and girls flippantly wrote, "Are you kidding?"

The brief list included these items: "My mom said she was glad I had a job because maybe I would stay out of trouble after school"; "My father thought it was a good idea I spent my own money to get my bicycle fixed"; praise for making a varsity athletic team; praise for getting a good grade.

We then queried the same parents about their adolescents, asking them to describe the qualities they valued and the qualities of which they disapproved. The positive characteristics were far fewer than the negative or disapproved of qualities. The same adults were asked if they made a practice of complimenting their youngsters for approved behaviors. One mother commented, "You mean every time my son doesn't hassle with his brother I'm supposed to compliment him? That's nonsense. He's seventeen. His brother is twelve. I'm not going to fall down on my knees just because he acts decently to his brother. He's older. He should know better."

In this instance the bickering between the two brothers had been causing considerable dissension in the house. Occasionally the arguments deteriorated into physical combat, which was even more annoying. We suggested she hold back completely on her criticism, her reminders not to pick on his younger brother. The first time she noticed the slightest behavior of the older boy that was positive toward his younger brother, she was to take notice and compliment him. Her reactions were to be private and brief. The reinforcement obviously had to take place more than just once. She agreed to try.

She complimented him privately about not tearing into his brother for playing some of his favorite records, borrowing a favorite shirt, using up all the hot water. As it turned out, her teenage son had not been consistently rude or hostile to his younger brother. It was simply that the mother was taking the positive things in the older boy's behavior for granted and focusing on the negative.

After several months of subtle, consistent complimenting of the older boy, he told his mother he had caught on to what she was doing. "Every time I don't lay into Jerry, you come up with some kind of you're wonderful stuff." He told her it had been a pretty neat sort of game to play and thought it was very amusing. It was more than just amusing, however, for the mother had made her point about his behavior, and the older boy had gained some insight into what he was doing that had been difficult for the family's relationship. The humor of the approach appealed to him. He also felt released from the feeling that his mother was always criticizing his every action, and most important, his behavior towards his younger brother had significantly changed for the better.

Whenever you can, hold off on your criticism. If you can't say something honestly positive, or at least neutral, it's probably best to keep quiet. When you see something that you disapprove of, assuming it's not really dangerous to anyone, remember that adolescents are extraordinarily changeable, and if you wait a little while, chances are that the behavior you disapprove of will disappear.

Parents sometimes slip into a position in which they can't seem to think or talk about anything other than the specific behavior or characteristic which they find objectionable at the time. Relationships become a tug of war; the adolescent digs his or her heels in and refuses to give up; the adult presses even harder with an onslaught of critical comments. Small things rapidly grow into major issues and everything else seems to be forgotten.

Jason and his father reached the point at which their relationship was nearly destroyed because Jason at age sixteen bought a gold hoop earring and started wearing it. The first time Jason's father saw the earring he demanded that his son immediately remove it. Jason refused.

Jason was forbidden to eat with the family; he was also told that unless the earring was removed, he would not be allowed to go with the family on vacation. Jason continued to resist. He liked the earring, he told his father.

Jason's father spoke to the school principal about having his son expelled from school. The guidance counselor and the principal agreed that the earring was objectionable, but in view of the relaxed codes regarding dress, the school couldn't officially expel him. Despite all negative reactions, Jason continued to wear the earring. One evening his father tried to pull the earring from Jason's ear. When Jason resisted, he and his father wrestled. Jason was forced to his knees; for the first time since Jason was a child, his father, usually a man of restraint, struck his son.

"I couldn't stand the earring," Jason's father told us. "Every time I came in at night I would take a look at this son of mine with an earring in one ear, and it finally got to me."

All of the boy's other qualities, the fact that he was a good-looking youngster, a good student involved in a wide range of activities, were forgotten because Jason's father was focusing on one ear. A piece of jewelry shadowed everything else his son did.

We talked with Jason about the quarrel. He told us that he had started wearing the earing as a joke. He never intended to keep it on permanently, but after his fther kept after him, he wasn't going to give in. He felt unhappy about their fight. He said that earlier that morning his father had asked him to clean out the garage.

"I cleaned the whole garage like he asked. He came home from work when I was finishing. He didn't even look at the garage. All he said was 'You're wearing that earring. This is the last time.' That's when he grabbed me and tried to pull the earring off."

In contrast to Jason's father, Sharon's mother curbed her obsession about her daughter's weight by using *selective vision*. Rather than bombard her daughter about curbing her appetite and dropping her newly-discovered hobby of cake baking, Sharon's mother made up her mind to concentrate on her daughter's good points. "I stopped seeing any of her between her neck and her knees," said Sharon's mother. She encouraged Sharon to let her hair grow long because the girl had lovely hair.

"I bought her barrettes, hats, fancy shoes and stockings. Every time she arranged her hair in a different way I noticed. I saw everything good about her. The one subject I refused to bring up was her weight. I remembered the times I had kept after her about losing weight, and all she would do was reach for another piece of cake."

Without exception, every teenager, boy or girl, goes through times of great concern about physical attractiveness. Sharon's bravado, reflected in her comment "I don't care if they call me fatty," masked her very real concern about her size. At this stage she didn't need the negative reinforcement from her mother. Through selective vision on her mother's part, Sharon could feel that she had some redeeming physical features. After months of selective vision, the pressure was off. Thus, when Sharon's mother finally made the comment that Sharon had so many attractive qualities, and she could be even *more* attractive if she lost weight, Sharon was the one to ask for help in going on a diet.

If you find that your adolescent is getting more and more stubborn, instead of beating your head against a stone wall, check on your own behavior. Perhaps your adolescent's stubbornness is at least a partly a defensive reaction to your criticism.

When parents focus on a behavior or characteristic of their adolescent that they disapprove of and the adolescent doesn't jump and change, parents are eager to label adolescents as stubborn. Putting a label on behavior doesn't explain anything. It's not a matter of stubbornness; the teenagers are reacting to the threat of adult criticism, and to maintain their own psychological integrity they have to resist changes others are trying to impose on them

When the criticisms stop, the behaviors often change. This is exactly what happened in Andrew's case. He refused to get a haircut. Thick and curly, his hair, a tangled mess, reached nearly to his shoulders. Neither parent could tolerate the sight of their son's hair.

"Facing him across a dinner table was enough to make me lose my appetite," commented his mother.

"The hair was repulsive," added Andrew's father. He couldn't understand why his son wouldn't listen to reason and "get the damn bush cut off."

Day after day they kept after him: "You look like you're

wearing a dish mop; you're going to get bugs growing; do you know what kind of impression you make on other people? No one wants to be seen with you."

Andrew had an answer to every comment: "It's my hair; I don't tell you the way to wear your hair; I don't care what other people think; if my hair makes you sick at supper, I can eat alone."

Any virtues Andrew had were lost in the conversations that were obsessed by hair. "It got to the point," his mother recalled, "that the minute I saw him I brought up his hair."

Andrew's parents finally realized that all of their nagging about his hair had no apparent effect on Andrew. If anything, the nagging made matters worse. Therefore, they stopped mentioning any subject remotely concerned with hair. "Sometimes he would just stand there facing me. I knew he was challenging me to say something. I never gave in."

During Andrew's senior year he had his photograph taken for the school yearbook. He brought home the proofs and told his parents he wasn't going to pay for them. According to Andrew the school had hired a "lousy photographer," and Andrew wasn't going to allow a distorted image to appear in the yearbook. His mother said the photograph was actually a good likeness. The print showed a part of a face and a lot of hair. Andrew insisted on going to another photographer. The results were the same.

A few weeks later, without saying a word to anyone in the family, Andrew came home with his hair cut. The next day he had his picture taken. "Aren't you going to say anything?" he asked his parents. With remarkable restraint, his mother remembers, she looked straight at her son and asked innocently, "About what?"

If you find that you have somehow slipped into a criti-

*cal, negative stance, that everything your adolescent
does seems to be wrong, there is only one thing to do
—stop the criticisms. At this point, criticizing can't do
anyone any good; it can only make things worse.*

You can't expect adolescents to break the chain of criticism; they're too busy defending themselves. Therefore, if anyone is going to break it, it has to be the parents. There isn't any secret about how to do this. If you find that you have slipped into a critical rut with your teenager, stop criticizing immediately—no matter how important you might feel the next criticism is going to be.

Adults sometimes fail to realize how sensitive to criticism most teenagers are. We have all gone through that period of hypersensitivity ourselves, but many of us have forgotten it. Remember that adolescents are going through a period of tremendous change and development. They are dealing with new social demands, new challenges, and they are sometimes very unsure of themselves. They may try to cover up with bravado, especially when relating to adults, but more often than not their main problem is a lack of self-confidence. Therefore, any minor criticism might take on extra emotional meaning, and from an adult's point of view the adolescent may seem to be overreacting to the most trivial comment.

We were having dinner with sixteen-year-old Carol and her parents. Carol got up from the table. Her boots scraped against the table's leg. "Here we go again," commented her mother. "Just once, Carol, can you get up without pounding your boots against the table?"

Carol's reaction was to get up from the table and leave the room in tears. "She's in the touchy stage," her mother said. "You look at her and she shouts, 'Why are you looking at me like that?' "

The mother viewed her own remark as an innocent, casual statement. Carol's behavior was irritating. No matter how often she was reminded, every time she got up from the table she kicked it. Carol felt that her mother was overly critical about everything. "Nothing I do is right." The statement about the boots triggered a whole range of associations about other events which had happened that day. She had misplaced her sweater, and her mother asked her if she had lost it. She had been reminded not to be forgetful. Without awareness, her mother had been guiding, judging, evaluating Carol about small matters. From Carol's perspective, they were major issues.

Tensions were considerably eased when Carol's mother asked herself, "Is this criticism really necessary?" every time she was ready to make a judgment about Carol's behavior. If the suggestion or criticism wasn't a matter of life or death, it was left unsaid. The vicious circle stopped. And the boots stopped scraping against the table.

In most instances it's best to simply overlook whatever minor things might seem wrong to us at the moment and try to focus on the positive. If you wait just a while, many of the little things the adolescent does that seem wrong to you will probably disappear without your saying anything about them.

Soap will go in the soap dish instead of lying over the drain melting away. Hair gets cut. Torn jeans and frayed sweaters are eventually discarded and replaced with jackets and slacks. (When the clothing bills arrive, you may even feel a bit of nostalgia about the good old economy days.) You can count on the natural changeability of adolescence to take care of most minor behavior problems.

Guidelines for Rational Parenting

The first step in learning to accentuate the positive is to

become more sensitive to the positive aspects of your adolescent's behavior. To increase your sensitivity in this direction, keep a diary of your adolescent's behavior for one week. Each night of the week, jot down everything your adolescent did that day that you consider a desirable bit of behavior. It needn't be anything major or monumental—just anything you view positively.

Now, whenever you notice something positive that your adolescent does, mention it. You don't have to make a big issue of your recognition, unless you feel it deserves some special praise. In most instances a smile, a word of recognition, perhaps just your tone of voice will convey the appropriate message.

At first, this pattern of accentuating the positive may seem artificial to you because most of us tend to be relatively neutral in our day-to-day interactions. Therefore, to guard against the possibility of injecting a sense of artificiality in your relationships, be absolutely honest in your praise. After a while, you will discover that you have started a positive cycle of interaction in which the recognition of your adolescent's appropriate behavior fosters and encourages similar behavior in the future. This benign atmosphere is far more important than achieving any particular behavior, and once this atmosphere becomes firmly established, you will find that accentuating the positive is a normal and natural part of everyday life with your adolescent.

Psychological Immunization

Psychologically immunize your adolescent against the real dangers of the world— but don't cry "Wolf."

"God help me if I had walked in to talk to my father with a cigarette in my mouth when I was sixteen," a woman in her middle forties commented. "Now I'd be grateful if I thought it was only cigarettes my kids are smoking."

Parents frequently describe their own past as an age of relative innocence when compared with today's teenage culture.

"Drive a car when I was my son's age? It was a big deal when I got to use the family car. The car meant our family ate. My father used it for business. He had a Depression mentality. Kids today can't even imagine what it was like in the 30's and 40's," said one man, father of a sixteen-year-old.

A mother of a seventeen-year-old daughter stated, "I only remember one girl in my high school who became pregnant. She wasn't allowed to stay in school. The girls were talking about her having a baby. I was sixteen. I asked, 'How did it happen?' Talk about innocence. My daughter tells me she is the only one in her group of friends who is *not* on the pill."

On the basis of what many adults say about their own adolescence, we might be tempted to conclude that parents of today's teenagers grew up in a sheltered, naive world. Obviously this is far from the truth. In every generation adolescents have had a variety of opportunities to get into trouble. As far as we can tell, that has always been part of growing up in our culture. However, it is probably true that the range of problems adolescents are likely to encounter has expanded over the past ten or fifteen years.

In a recent survey we asked parents of varying educational and socioeconomic backgrounds to list their major concerns about their adolescent youngsters. A variety of fears, concerns, and worries were cited, but the four consistently mentioned by parents in all walks of life were drugs, sex, alcohol, and cars.

They worry about drugs. Typical comments:

"I live in constant fear my kid will get hooked on drugs. He has one friend now up on a drug charge."

"My son tells me they sell joints in the schoolyard like they were selling candy in my day."

They worry about alcohol:

"We had parties when I was a kid. Parents stayed in the house. They served soft drinks. My daughter gave a party. These two boys walked over to my husband and asked him where the liquor was. He was ready to throw them out of the house."

"Fourteen-year-old kids. Babies. My son said there was beer at the party—all the beer kids could drink. What am I going to do? Lock my boy up in a glass cage? He tells me there's nothing wrong because the other boys and girls drink beer. It's the same excuse—the other kids do it, so that makes it right."

They worry about early sexual experiences that may have traumatic consequences. The father of a teenage daughter and son remarked, "You're damn right I have a double standard. I don't want my daughter sleeping around. I don't ask my son questions. I can't see it the same way with my daughter. I told her she'd be a fool to let herself be taken advantage of. She'll be the one hurt.''

A mother of a teenage girl stated, "I'm certainly all in favor of women's lib, and then I have this gut reaction when I think about my daughter. She's too young. It bothers me a lot—the stories I hear. Her friends having sex. I know what's going on, and I get uptight when it comes to my daughter. She's too young. I don't think she's had sex, but I can't be sure. I'm part of another generation in my values."

And parents worry about the possibility of automobile accidents, especially when their teenager might be under the influence of alcohol or some other drug.

These four sources of danger do not by any means exhaust the list of worries parents express, but they are clearly the most common and they illustrate the kinds of concerns many parents may have. We don't have to be paranoid to recognize that there are real dangers in the world; and when these dangers are considered in conjunction with the adolescent's healthy drive to explore the world, we can readily appreciate parents' concerns.

Because of the very serious consequences that might result from their adolescents' explorations, parental concern can easily grow beyond realistic proportions. We have to realize, therefore, that only a very small percentage of adolescents ever develop a serious drug problem, though even this small percentage represents a terrible tragedy in our society. We must also recognize that despite the popular and more lurid reports in newspapers and magazines, life for the great majority of adolescents is very far from the wild sex orgy some writers have pictured it to be. And we must also remember that, by and large, most adolescents are at least as good drivers as their parents are. Nevertheless, it would be foolish to discount entirely the real dangers that adolescents do in fact meet.

The parent of a teenager who does have a drug problem, the parent whose child has been hurt by a sexual experience, the parent of an adolescent who has had an automobile accident isn't concerned about statistics. The suffering felt by both parent and teenager is not reduced one iota when someone points out that the adolescent is one of a very small percentage who have a particular problem. Regardless of statistics, the potential dangers and the possible suffering are undeniably real.

But what can parents do to deal most effectively with their concerns? They obviously cannot, and certainly should not, prevent their adolescent from encountering the realities of the world outside the home and family. Efforts to overprotect a teenager in this way can only lead to rebellion or to a kind of schizoid existence that is in some respects worse than the dangers against which the parent is trying to protect the adolescent.

Overprotection goes hand-in-hand with nagging, and while parents may recognize that overprotection doesn't work very well, most of us still seem to have faith in the value of nagging. Unfortunately, that faith is often misplaced, as the following examples illustrate. We queried a large group of teenagers about their knowledge of the effects of drugs. One question was about parental input. What had their parents said or done to dissuade them from drug experimentation?

"Has your mother or father talked to you about drugs?" we asked one seventeen-year-old boy.

His response, typical of the majority we heard, was "Yeah."

"What was told to you?"

"Don't take drugs."

"Anything else?"

"She said I'd be making trouble for myself and for her."

"Any other information?"

"Maybe a hundred times I hear her—the same thing. You better not take drugs."

"How about your reaction? Did that stop you?"

"No."

"Can you think of why?"

He looked puzzled. "She's got a no for everything I want to do. All she says is no. I don't listen to her anymore. Don't get me wrong. I get along fine with her."

Constant nagging is worse than useless. It not only does little or no good in protecting the adolescent, but it also is likely to disrupt the entire relationship between parent and teenager. Indeed, parental nagging may very well provoke the adolescent into behaving in precisely the way the parents are so worried about.

In talking with teenagers about the forms of parental instruction they received, the most frequently mentioned technique was lecturing (another form of nagging). Specifically, this meant that at some inopportune time, such as when the teenager was ready to leave the house or right after dinner when plans had been made to meet a friend, a parent corners the adolescent and demands to emphasize a point. The voices rise, and when the teenager gives the slightest hint of making a comment, the parental voice booms, "Don't interrupt me. Wait until I'm finished, damn it. You're going to listen. Then I'll see if you have anything to say."

What was the reaction of the teenagers? "I turn off," one boy told us. Our own son reacted somewhat differently. Just as his father was getting warmed up for what promised to be a long and instructive lecture, our son grabbed a pencil and paper.

"What the hell are you doing?"

"Taking notes for the exam."

"You put down the paper and listen."

Parents get carried away by the sounds of their own voices in these lecturing sessions. They use every dramatic technique; their voices may never have been so resonant. Unfortunately, the captive audience, the teenagers forced to listen, have an escape route—their own private fantasies. And they waken only at the final lines.

"Were you listening?"

"Sure, Dad."

"Okay. What did I say?"

"About what?"

None of us likes to be lectured at, even when it is ostensibly "for our own good," and adolescents are no different in this respect from the rest of humanity. To achieve a psychological innoculation against the potential evils that will have a meaningful effect over time, there must be a give-and-take between adult and adolescent, an honest sharing of information, opinions, and points of view. If there is disagreement, there should be freedom to disagree openly, without the threat of later punishment.

"You're wrong, Dad. You're wrong. What do you know about pot? You don't know anything about it."

Every parent has heard some variation of these words, and the parent's reaction is typically, "Don't sit there and tell me I'm wrong. Don't you dare talk to me like that!"

The battle lines are drawn, and the youngster and parent are set up as adversaries. However, there can't be a winner or loser in such situations—only losers.

While most parents are aware of the dangers their adolescents might encounter, they often feel frustrated by their inability to do anything constructive. They've probably tried nagging and found that that doesn't work very well. From time to time they may have issued emotional warnings to their adolescent that certain kinds of behavior will not be tolerated, but most parents feel that these warnings fall on deaf ears. Consequently, many parents seem to operate under the assumption that "it can't happen to us." They play ostrich, hoping that their teenagers will be wise enough— and most important, lucky enough—to stay out of any serious difficulties. If serious problems do arise, they are often astonished.

"I never dreamed my child would get into trouble," a woman told us. "She's had everything she's wanted. She's been a good girl—naive, if anything." Her daughter was pregnant, and the mother found it difficult to believe her daughter had even had sex. In this instance, playing ostrich and trusting to luck was obviously not enough. Parents certainly can and must do more to help their adolescents.

By the time children become adolescents, they have developed the capacity to imagine future situations and anticipate future possibilities. This is the basis of foresight, and by virtue of our capacity for foresight, we are able to think ahead, plan for the future, develop tentative solutions to potential problems—in short, behave like intelligent human beings.

Foresight is also the basis for *psychologically immunizing* the adolescent against the real dangers of the world.

Psychological immunization works in much the same way as physical innoculation meant to protect the child from small pox, diphtheria, polio, or any other physical illness. Before the child encounters these diseases in the real world, a small amount of toxin and antitoxin is injected, and this injection stimulates the production of antibodies, which immunize the child against a particular disease. Similarly, in psychological immunization, we introduce the adolescent to a particular danger by thinking ahead together, relying on the imaginative capacity for foresight to stimulate the development of attitudes, values, and habits that will immunize the adolescent against the danger when it is encountered in the world outside of the home. The parents' job is to "inject" some information, some evidence, some question of choice that will start the process of psychological immunization. But the final "antibodies," the values, attitudes, and choices that will ultimately guide future behavior, must be "produced" by the adolescents themselves.

A parent with whom we discussed the process of thinking together retorted, "You don't know adolescents. What I say goes in one ear and out the other. Kids live from day to day. My daughter can't see ahead. She doesn't think about the consequences of what she does."

In several meetings we had with the daughter, a totally different picture emerged. The girl worried constantly about herself and her place in her peer group. She was afraid of saying no and suffering rejection from her friends. She had tried pot and didn't like the experience, but some of her companions had been pressuring her to continue. She didn't want to and didn't know how to go about breaking off with her old group. She worried about what she was going to do in her life. Was it too late for her to work hard to get her grades up so she could get into college? She hesitated to talk with her mother about her worries because she knew her mother would discount her worries. "My mom always tells me that I have it easy. She says I won't know what problems really are until I get older."

Unfortunately, parents tend either to dismiss teenagers' concerns as not really serious or to rely on old-fashioned "hell-and-damnation" lectures reminiscent of their own early lives. Instead of haranguing the teenager about the eternal price of sin and the importance of a rather abstract code of morals, effective psychological immunization relies primarily on facts, information, evidence that derives from the concrete world of reality. Thus, psychologically immunizing against exposure to the dangers of drugs must depend upon valid information about drug usage and specific evidence about the consequences. Exhortations to lead a good life or to beware of the consequences of sin may evoke some temporary feelings of guilt, but for most adolescents these kinds of exhortations have little or no effect.

When you are trying to innoculate your teenager against some specific potential danger, rely primarily on facts, information, and evidence. Be as concrete as you can and stay away from abstract discussions of sin and morality.

Effective immunization also depends upon thinking ahead *together*. The adolescent isn't immunized by being lectured at; the only gain from these one-way parental lectures is the feeling of satisfaction parents might get from doing a job they think they are supposed to do. But this satisfaction is often short-lived when parents realize that their stirring lectures have stirred only themselves.

Listening to what the teenager has to say is the critical next step. Responding to the comment "You're wrong, Dad, you're wrong" with a sincerely open attitude is a far better parental tactic than lecturing or nagging.

"Why am I wrong? I'd really like to know."

Whatever the topic—pot, sex, alcohol, cars—giving the teenager a chance to express opinions, even if the opinions at first seem absurd, leaves the door open for both parents and adolescents to explore and share their views.

198 PSYCHOLOGICAL IMMUNIZATION

Most important is the opportunity to communicate, to learn the facts associated with a potentially dangerous situation, to explore alternative choices, to think together about possible consequences, to discover one's own values and the values of significant other persons.

Remember that the process of effective innoculation involves parent and adolescent thinking together— sharing information, opinions, experiences, and points of view. Avoid one-way lectures in which you try to impose your views on your teenager.

Don't expect an explicit, hard-and-fast conclusion from such discussions. Remember that you can sometimes lead adolescents to a conclusion, but you can't force them to draw the conclusion—and really believe it. In fact, most successful immunizing conversations never come to a specific conclusion, and the adult may wonder if anything has been achieved. There can never be a guarantee of success, but keep in mind that forcing an adolescent to mouth some artificial promise about future behavior is almost bound to lead to failure. Much more effective immunization is likely to take place if adolescents have a chance to think about what they have learned, what they have shared, and then draw their own conclusions.

Leave the innoculating conversation open-ended; let the adolescents draw their own conclusions. Your responsibility as a parent is to get the process started and help move it along. You cannot develop in the adolescent the attitudes, values, and habits that will provide effective immunity; only the adolescents themselves can do that, so give them a chance to come to their own conclusions and develop their own immunizing strengths.

In introducing information about a potentially dangerous

situation, a parent has to be careful about arousing too much fear and anxiety in the adolescent. If a situation is portrayed in extraordinarily shocking terms, it is liable to make the adolescent increasingly defensive and resistant to change. Or, it may present the potential danger as a challenge, a dare that is too exciting to avoid. This will defeat the goal of immunization. Rather than trying to innoculate the adolescent by fright, a technique that is often not very effective in the long run and may have results quite different from those planned, parents are much more likely to achieve the goals of innoculation by sticking to the facts and letting the facts speak for themselves, without excessive emotional input.

"You take drugs. You'll ruin your life. That's the end. You'll wind up in jail!"

"I'm warning you. You drive the car at those speeds and you know what'll happen?—you'll be in a hospital bed. That'll be the end of your playing ball."

"You get pregnant and you'll be the one who suffers. You think you can go to school with a baby at seventeen years of age? You fool around and you'll be sorry the rest of your life."

Through fear tactics parents risk setting up a dare. "Go ahead and try but . . ." and the temptation to taste the forbidden becomes too hard to resist. "Will it really turn out that way?" thinks the teenager. The consequences seem remote, and he or she focuses on the process, which may have strong appeal.

Be careful about arousing too much fear and anxiety. Shock tactics can sometimes backfire and defeat a parent's purpose.

Like most other aspects of parenting, the timing of innoculations is crucial. If a parent begins worrying about some particular danger too early in the adolescent's life and introduces the topic for the purpose of innoculation, there will probably be little positive benefit. In fact, parents run the risk of negative consequences.

One adolescent girl who worried about her relationship with boys remembered the day she began menstruating for the first time. Her mother sat down with her and talked about not letting boys take advantage of her because now she could become pregnant. A kiss from a boy threw her into a panic, even though she knew that was absurd.

The dangerous situation must be a realistic possibility for the adolescent at the time it is discussed; otherwise, talking about it will have little personal meaning for the adolescent, and the process of immunization will not take hold.

But just as parents can introduce a topic too soon, they can also begin the process too late to be fully effective. The moment at which a crisis occurs is clearly *not* an opportune time for the parent to sit down and begin reviewing the facts about possible dangers. The adolescent has already encountered them. At the time of crisis, more than anything else the adolescent needs unqualified, unquestioning, and total support of parents. Issues of innoculation against future dangers must be put aside to deal with immediate concerns.

Timing is important. Don't try to immunize your child against some potential danger before that danger is a possibility in your child's life. And don't attempt the immunization process when a crisis has emerged: Psychological innoculations are most successful when the danger is a meaningful possibility for the teenager and before a crisis has developed.

Parents must also accept the fact that they cannot immunize their teenagers against all the possible dangers in the world. To attempt that would be useless and self-defeating.

Repeated parental warnings about one potential danger after another lead most adolescents into a state of selective deafness: Moreoever, there is no need to deal with every specific danger imaginable. Successful innoculations tend to be general in the sense that the values, attitudes, and habits that protect an adolescent from one particular kind of danger also work to protect them from other kinds of difficulties.

Finally, parents must never cry "Wolf!" unless there is a real "wolf" to worry about. Efforts to immunize teenagers against dangers that are trivial or unrealistic undermine the effects of all future innoculations. The teenager soon learns to distrust any parental warning or concern, even if some of the parental worries are legitimate. Parents must therefore be selective in their innoculating efforts, and above all, they must always deal with realistic dangers that their teenagers will eventually recognize as valid problems.

Be selective in your immunization efforts, and never cry "Wolf." Always be sure that the danger you are concerned about is, in fact, a real danger.

With judicious timing, some patience, and understanding, parents can reasonably prepare their teenagers for the problems they are most likely to meet.

Guidelines for Rational Parenting

Your first step in psychological innoculation is selecting which specific dangers you most want to protect your adolescent against. If you tried to protect your adolescent against every possible danger he or she might run into, the process of psychological immunization would become a full-time enterprise, and you would discover that its effectiveness rapidly decreased. So focus on a problem that you are sure is real and one that will be meaningful to your adolescent.

Remember that effective innoculation must be solidly based on facts. Do some research. Don't rely on what you've heard in casual conversations or gossip. Take the time and energy necessary to learn the basic facts relevant to the problem. Use your local library as a resource to find out what information is available. If the problem you're concerned about concerns drugs, alcohol, driving, sexual activities, or smoking, seek out local organizations concerned with each of these issues and ask for any printed information available. Talk to a qualified expert on the matter to discover what is known about the problem. However you go about it, get the facts.

In beginning to discuss the potential problem with your adolescent, select a time which is convenient to both of you. You don't want to feel hurried and you don't want to be interrupted, so be sure you both have plenty of time.

In presenting the problem, don't pussyfoot around it. Be straightforward and matter-of-fact. Express your concern directly and present the facts—all of the facts you know, not just those that happen to support your view.

Then listen. Give your adolescent plenty of opportunity to react without getting into a debate. If you present the facts without attacking your adolescent, more often than not you will discover that he or she is also aware of the possible dangers and has probably thought about them. Listen empathetically, trying to get a sense of how your adolescent sees the problem.

In the course of talking *with* your adolescent, make your own opinions clear and explicit, but be sure you present them as *your* opinions, not as the only *right* answers. Take special care not to slip into the role of either prosecuting attorney or moralizer.

After you and your adolescent have had a chance to review

the facts and share opinions, let matters rest. Don't push for a promise or a neat resolution. Take a chance on your adolescent's own sense of values and potential for maturity.

Remember that no matter what you say, if your behavior contradicts what you say, the chances of your achieving successful immunization with your teenager are likely to be greatly reduced. If adolescents sometimes fail to pay attention to parental words, they rarely fail to notice parental behavior, so what you *do* is likely to have greater impact than what you *say*.

Expectations

*Expect adolescents to behave maturely
and chances are they will.*

All of us are influenced by the expectations of other people. In schools, for example, researchers have found that if teachers expect their students to perform poorly on various learning tasks, by and large the students will not learn as much as when their teachers expect their students to perform well.

Exactly the same process operates in relations between parents and their adolescents. A parent who expects a teenager to be immature demands less from the teenager, sets relatively low goals, and probably rewards less mature behavior. Even more important is the unspoken message that is conveyed to the teenager. Without coming out and saying it openly, the parent with low expectations is nevertheless communicating to the adolescent a message that says, "I don't expect much from you because you are immature, a child, a person who is not grown up." As a result, adolescents treated this way by their parents learn to see themselves as immature, and indeed tend to behave immaturely. This kind of self-fulfilling prophecy was a major factor in creating the problems faced by a fifteen-year-old boy with whom we worked.

Paul, a round-faced, husky youngster, was known as "Baby." He'd been given the nickname at birth by his four-year-old brother, who'd had difficulty pronouncing the initial P in Paul's name. To avoid saying "Paul," the brother called him "Baby." The name stuck. Paul was "Baby" at home and "Baby" to classmates. The name, coy and amusing when Paul was a toddler, became a problem when Paul was a fifteen-year-old high school sophomore and still seemed to be behaving like a much younger child.

His mother was irritated when the school's guidance counselor requested a meeting. "There's nothing wrong with my son. He's an intelligent, serious boy." She felt that the school had unfairly labeled her son a problem simply because he didn't conform to the aggressive, tough behaviors of his peer group.

The counselor explained that Paul's teachers saw him as immature; he frequently behaved childishly, and that because of this immaturity he was rejected by his classmates.

"It doesn't make sense to me. Paul has friends. I know that for a fact. He has boys over at the house," his mother indicated.

"He doesn't relate to youngsters at school," the counselor responded.

"What difference does that make? I don't see why he has to limit himself to kids at school. I don't think it's the school's business who he is friends with."

The counselor insisted that the school was concerned about Paul and the effects his behavior had on his self-image. He became upset when rejected, and he behaved childishly to attract attention. He was dependent on the teachers, hovering near their desks, remaining after class, arriving early and using other attention-getting mechanisms. He made no effort to relate to his classmates.

Paul, the youngest of four children, had received a great deal of attention from his family. Because of the gap in ages between him and the other children, his parents tended to handle him differently. As a baby he was more often carried than taken in a carriage or a stroller. When babysitting for Paul, his older brothers and sister kept him in a playpen long after he was able to get around on his own. When Paul was old enough to attend kindergarten, his sister or brothers took him to school. Eager to leave in the morning, impatient with his struggles to dress himself, get his shoes on and laces correctly tied, they found it easier to do the tasks for him. Paul's mother confessed that of all her children, it had been the hardest for her to see Paul growing up. She repeatedly found herself having what she termed that "only yesterday feeling" about him. "It seems such a short time ago that I brought him home from the hospital. He was an adorable baby."

She couldn't wait for the others to get out of diapers, off to school, and on their own. "I seemed less in a hurry about Paul. I always let him do things at his own pace. I think of the walkers I bought for the others. We pushed them into bicycles. We didn't worry about Paul. I guess we knew that eventually he would be dry at night, walk, and talk. It didn't matter whether it was a month or two months more. He wasn't in the way. My other kids were good with him."

If he complained about being mistreated by his siblings, his mother intervened and stopped the bickering and fighting. "Paul is a baby—he's much younger. Don't pick on your brother."

When Paul was fourteen, his parents were divorced. By that time the other children were living away from home, but Paul remained with his mother. "It hasn't been easy. We don't have help and I'm working."

Despite Paul's awareness of their situation, there was a wide gap between Paul's sense of obligation to his mother and his performance. "He tries," his mother said, but it was clear that Paul didn't fulfill his responsibilities at home.

Paul's mother found that either she did things herself or they didn't get done. She said that she tried to get after Paul "in spurts," but most of the time she found it easier to walk the dog, shop, prepare dinner, and do the other household chores herself.

Her excuse was that Paul, more than the other children, had a lot to contend with emotionally after the divorce. "The rest were away, beginning their own lives. Paul was home. He's still a baby. I tell myself, what difference does it make whether he takes his jacket to the cleaners or I do? He's still young. He'll have a lifetime to do these things. Does it really matter that he begins at fifteen, sixteen? Before I know it, he'll be off to college like the others, and then he can manage."

The first thing we noticed about Paul was his appearance. He seemed to look much younger than fifteen, and the contrast between his deep voice, his large vocabulary, and his round face with undefined features was striking. The innocence of his expression, the impish quality to his face, seemed a perfect fit for his nickname, "Baby."

We asked him how he felt about the name.

"It doesn't matter. People call me what they like. I'm used to it."

"How about your classmates?"

"I don't care."

"Do they call you Baby?"

"Mostly behind my back. Some to my face."

Paul insisted that he liked the name. It was familiar and his brothers and sister called him "Baby," though he objected when his father called him "Big Baby."

"He thinks I'm lazy."

"How do you mean?"

"He says that if my head wasn't screwed on, I'd lose it.

He got pissed off because I took his umbrella and forgot to bring it back. I can't find it.''

Paul went on to explain that his mother had started to react similarly, complaining about his forgetfulness and lack of responsibility. ''She wants me to jump if she asks me to do something. I'd get around to doing it if she would leave me alone.''

He also said that when he did carry out his mother's orders, she was never satisfied. ''Like when I cleaned up the kitchen when she had to go out. She got home and the first thing she asked me was whether I put cleanser in the sink.''

Paul seemed fairly content with himself and also content to let his mother take care of his belongings, remind him of his appointments, and generally take care of him. But he was concerned that his teachers didn't like him, and he couldn't understand why. ''Other kids hang around and ask questions, and when I do, they tell me I have to find the answers for myself.'' He couldn't understand their rejection.

In talking with his teachers, the consistent reaction was that Paul was very childish. One teacher commented that she had the feeling she was addressing a ten-year-old boy. ''He is very dependent, clinging, reminds me of a child in the third grade who constantly needs direction. I don't think it's because he really does need that kind of guidance. He has the *need* to ask for help.''

Paul's immaturity was partly a result of some long-term problems in his family, and also due to other factors, such as his physical appearance. But a central theme throughout his life was his family's view of Paul as a baby. He was *expected* to be immature, and partly as a result of these expectations, Paul behaved immaturely.

Check your perceptions of your adolescents, your expectations of their behavior. Do you expect them to

behave immaturely and thus treat them as immature
people?

Fortunately, expectations work both ways. Just as expecting immaturity often leads to immature behavior, as in Paul's case, expecting maturity may lead to more mature behavior.

Justin's parents were divorced when he was fifteen. His mother was awarded custody of Justin and his ten-year-old sister. Because of the age difference between the two children, Justin and his sister had led completely independent lives. Justin had never participated in taking care of his sister. He had his own friends and his own social life. There had been no demands on his time for baby-sitting, taking his sister out for an afternoon. His mother had always relied on outside help.

The divorce radically changed the home situation. Justin's mother returned to work. She could no longer afford the luxury of sitters, and there were days when she couldn't get home for her daughter after school.

As she reported, Justin discovered his sister at age fifteen. To save his mother worry, he made it a point to meet his sister at her school and bring her home. On weekends, realizing his mother was tired, he took his sister to the movies. In any number of small ways, his mother reported, Justin made an effort to be an older brother and to help out. It wasn't that Justin "jumped in" and assumed these responsibilities. What surprised his mother was his effort and willingness when she talked to him about the situation. "I let him know I needed him. His sister wouldn't be ten forever. It would be just a few years before she, too, was old enough to take care of herself. Right now I needed his help, and he understood. He's done what he can. I don't expect miracles. I don't want him to give up his life—just help out to ease things with her in the present situation.''

Naturally, merely expecting mature behavior doesn't mean that an adolescent will automatically and necessarily become mature. As any parent can testify, few things in a teenager's life occur automatically or necessarily. It's a matter of increasing the likelihood of mature behavior, not guaranteeing that maturity will suddenly appear when parents expect it.

If your expectations are unrealistic, work at bringing them into line with reality. At first, changing your expectations may seem to be artificial and mechanical, but remember that expecting adolescents to be mature increases the likelihood of their behaving maturely.

To understand the influence of parental expectations, we must consider the ways in which teenagers view themselves, their self-concepts. Very early in life each person begins to develop some sense of self. At first this self-awareness is primarily in terms of physical sensations (*I* am hot; *I* am cold; *I* am hungry), but as the child grows older, other kinds of experiences contribute more and more to the person's sense of self.

By far the most important of these experiences occurs in the child's relationships with significant other people, and unquestionably the most significant others are the child's parents. Largely as a result of the hundreds and eventually thousands of interactions between the child and significant other people, the child develops a sense of "Who I am." Thus, the child's self-concept is learned in a social context and reflects the way others have behaved in relationship to the child. As a general rule, the child who has been treated as an intelligent person comes to view himself or herself as valuable. In other words, to a large extent our self-concepts are reflections of the way others have related to us.

During the later part of childhood, from the age of about nine or ten to thirteen or fourteen, the child's self-concept remains fairly stable. Some changes occur, of course, with the child's daily experiences at home, in school, and at play, but for the most part the general outlines of the child's self-concept are set and not easily altered. With the onset of puberty, however, adolescents' views of themselves and the ways in which they think about themselves become much more susceptible to change. These changes are initiated by the physical development that takes place at this time, but just as it was in the process of developing self-concept in early childhood, relationships with significant others become increasingly powerful in influencing adolescents' views of themselves. Thus, parents' expectations as they are expressed in interactions with their teenagers have a tremendous impact on the teenager's self-concept.

This impact is reflected not only in the way teenagers view themselves, but also in their behavior. Learning to behave as an adult, learning to accept the responsibilities and meet the standards of adulthood depends partly upon learning to think of oneself as an adult and having the confidence to act in ways that fit a mature self-image. A parent who expects an adolescent to behave maturely inevitably reflects this expectation in interacting with the teenager. As a result, the teenager is likely to develop a mature self-concept and to behave more maturely in an effort to fulfill that image.

Don't just tell teenagers to grow up and act like adults. Instead treat them more like adults and you'll be much more successful in helping them mature.

Simply telling a teenager to grow up and act like an adult has little or no effect, except perhaps to start an argument. But if parents actually treat teenagers as mature people, chances are that teenagers will come to see themselves as mature and consequently behave more maturely.

This was our aim in working with Paul and his mother. We tried to help Paul's mother see him as a young man instead of as a "baby" and thus begin in Paul a cycle of increasing psychological maturity. Her specific task was to shift responsibilities to Paul, responsibilities with which he could realistically cope. The responsibilities had to be meaningful, not artificially created. And thus, Paul began with concrete tasks, such as making sure there was milk and cereal in the house. We were careful not to overwhelm him by forcing him to take a sudden, giant step into maturity, but rather to let him develop gradually, step-by-step, into a more responsible and mature person. The crucial difference, however, was not in the specific tasks assigned to Paul, but rather in his mother's general attitude toward him.

We encouraged her to let Paul make his own decisions whenever possible. For example, she gave Paul the money to buy a winter jacket of his own choosing. This was a very meaningful experience for Paul. His mother reported that he told everyone they knew about buying his own jacket himself. Paul was eager to grow up, and without the earlier expectations that had blocked his development, Paul made rapid progress towards maturity. By helping Paul's mother change her expectations about Paul, by helping her see her son as a young man rather than as a child, we helped her change her view of Paul. This in turn caused Paul's own view of himself to change, and his behavior changed accordingly.

Expectations are not a magic potion for gaining immediate maturity in one's children, but if parents are concerned about their teenagers' immature behaviors, they should carefully examine their own views to determine the degree to which their teenagers' immaturity reflects parental expectations and parental behavior toward them. Some changes in these expectations might very well be warranted. As parents change their expectations, begin to view their teenagers as more mature and treat them more maturely, their teenagers are likely to see themselves as more mature and indeed behave more maturely.

Don't expect changes overnight; be patient and consistent.

Parents shouldn't expect their teenagers to mature all at once; changes take time and require patience and consistency on the part of parents. Moreover, parental expectations must be reasonable and realistic; otherwise, both parents and adolescents will be frustrated. If parents err, however, it is better to err on the side of expecting greater maturity from their adolescents rather than less, so as to encourage and reinforce the teenager's inherent capacity for psychological growth.

The problem of expectations is reflected most dramatically, perhaps, by family labels that some people carry with them. Labels get assigned surprisingly early in life. "He's my serious child," a mother told us. "My daughter is the happy one." And thus, practically from infancy on, this mother had two children clearly labeled—one serious and one happy. No wonder their mother was shocked when later in childhood her "serious one" acted up and the "happy one" regularly dissolved into tears. Many of us recall labels assigned to us by parents or members of our extended family.

Be careful of labels and nicknames. If you do choose a descriptive nickname for your child, be sure to pick out one that emphasizes an attribute that will be desirable later on in the child's life.

"She's my slow child," one mother told us. "My other two are very quick in learning to do anything; Linda is the slow one in everything she tries to do." The three children had been signed up to attend our summer camp. Linda, the slow one, was fourteen; Jimmy the "devil," was twelve; and Sue, the "little actress," was nine. We were accustomed to hearing such labels for children. In running a children's camp for over twenty years and working with hundreds of children, we had run across many such labels.

The "slow one" was assigned to a bunk with girls her own age. Linda was the *first* in her group to pass a swimming test. Linda, the slow one, should have been last.

It is inevitable in a summer camp that a counselor leaves early in the season or a junior counselor doesn't work out. There's a mad scramble to find a replacement. That summer the junior counselor in a younger bunk went home. Linda had become friends with the counselor and asked if she could help out for a while. She took over a variety of tasks— bedtime reading, helping the children dress for swimming, making their campfires. On visiting day the mother was stunned.

"You trusted her?" we were asked with obvious astonishment.

Fortunately for Linda, the information about her being slow had been filed away in the office cabinets. In the rush of managing a children's camp, we hadn't had time to check the application forms and find out that Responsible Linda was supposed to be Slow Linda, and so, Linda had escaped the expectations set up by her family label.

Guidelines for Rational Parenting

Set aside some time when you won't be interrupted and you can be free to reflect about what you expect from your adolescent. Because this question often leads to a fairly complicated answer, you may wish to write down your ideas. Don't be at all concerned about any logical order in your thinking or whether the expectations you think of make sense to you. Simply write down everything you think of, without censoring your thoughts to make them seem reasonable or "look good."

You may want to begin with your expectations regarding the routine of daily living—helping with household chores, taking care of his or her room, clothes, and so on. Jot down whatever comes to mind, no matter how trivial it may seem. Then, let your thoughts roam into other areas of life—education, family relationships, economic responsibilities, long-term goals—and write down all of the expectations you can think of.

After you have finished your list, leave it alone for a day or two, and then pick it up again and read through it. What have you left out? What else occurs to you?

At this point you should have a fairly comprehensive list that makes explicit the expectations you have about your adolescent, ranging from everyday matters to long-term life goals. Now, go through your list and consider each of the expectations you've written down. For each one, answer two questions for yourself.

1. Is this expectation realistic? Can I reasonably expect my teenager at the present time and in the present circumstances to fulfill this expectation?
2. Is this an expectation that encourages maturity on the part of my adolescent? Or is this an expectation that may foster immaturity and block psychological growth?

On the basis of this review you should have a comprehensive understanding of what you expect from your adolescent. You can now consider the question of how well your adolescent fulfills each of your expectations. For the sake of convenience, go through your list one by one, and next to each expectation, jot down your opinion of how well your adolescent fulfills that expectation, using a simple rating scale: (1) Okay; (2) Not so okay; (3) A problem.

After you have had plenty of time to think about this general issue yourself and have had a chance to clarify your thoughts, share the results of your thinking with your adolescent. In approaching this topic, don't beat around the bush. Tell your adolescent what you have been thinking about, and indicate that you want to share the results of your thinking, not for the sake of argument but so that both of you can gain greater understanding of what is going on between you.

Talk together about the expectations you have listed. Consider the question of whether each expectation is realistic or unrealistic, whether each tends to encourage or discourage maturity, and the degree to which you feel your adolescent meets your expectations. Be careful not to turn this into a lecture or an argument. Try to be as matter-of-fact as you can. In both what you say and how you say it, emphasize that you are merely reporting your thoughts and opinions, not building up a case either for or against yourself or your adolescent.

And then, *listen* to your adolescent's reaction. Have you left out any expectations that are important from your adolescent's perspective? What is your adolescent's view of how realistic your expectations are? How does your adolescent feel about whether your expectations tend to encourage or discourage maturity? What are your adolescent's evaluations of the degree to which he or she actually fulfills or should fulfill your expectations?

Remember that you are not trying to eliminate the expectations you have about your adolescent. That would be psychologically unrealistic because all of us inevitably have expectations about one another. But on the basis of your increased awareness of your own expectations and your empathetic understanding of your adolescent's reactions, you can modify your expectations to make them more realistic. And with your adolescent you can work toward changing some of these expectations in a direction that is more likely to foster your adolescent's increasing maturity.

Mutual Enjoyment

*Do things together that both you
and your adolescent enjoy.*

When our first child was born, we bought a camera and
began a photo record of his early years. The practice continued with the second youngster, and thus, in the dozen or so
photographic albums we have on a living room bookshelf,
the first eight contain one photo after another of happy
family shots. There are naked one-year-olds on isolated
beaches waving at distant sea gulls; toddlers sitting in toy
cars; six-year-olds with hair carefully brushed, ready for their
first day of grade school; children chasing kites in the park,
family picnics, camel rides in the local zoo. All are part of a
vivid record of fun and games. We're a happy, contented-
foursome doing just about anything and everything for the
sole purpose of enjoyment.

It's quite obvious from later albums, however, that by the
time the boys reached adolescence, parenting had become a
serious business. First of all, these volumes contain more
scenic shots than family pictures. Volumes 9, 10, and 11 have
dozens of empty pages. The few photos we have of our
children between the years of thirteen and eighteen provide
a startling contrast with the pictures of the early years. A
fifteen-year-old doesn't smile at the camera. More often
than not it had taken a considerable amount of coercion to
get our adolescents in front of a camera, and if there were
smiles, they were either forced or, worse yet, expressions
which can best be described as smirks.

Family life as represented in the albums reveals the disturbing but very real fact that parenting in adolescence had taken on a solemn note. We're not "caught on film" splashing in the lakes, riding sleds down snow-covered slopes. We're not cuddled together on a blanket on the beach. When our adolescents wanted to enjoy themselves, they sought out their own friends as companions.

Relationship with our adolescents, for the most part, involved chores, responsibilities, problems, conflicts—all the business of living without an equal amount of enjoyment. Obviously this didn't mean that we suddenly stopped doing things together; however, the times for carefree fun and games which were plentiful in their early childhood became less and less frequent. We didn't plan our lives this way. The natural aging process of both our children and ourselves was responsible. After all, when a boy is six, playing baseball with a parent is still a challenge. But when he is sixteen, playing catch with a parent will hardly strike him as the most pleasurable way to spend a spring afternoon.

Many parents, like ourselves, slip into a pattern of serious, heavy-handed interactions with their youngsters without being aware of a change. Nevertheless, this shift has emotional consequences. When the relationship between parent and adolescent becomes focused primarily on the business of living, to the exclusion of anything that might be done together just for enjoyment, the relationship cannot help but take on a serious tone. After a while, without thinking about it, both parent and teenager automatically slip into a sober emotional stance in relating to each other. They become problem-oriented, ready to interpret whatever occurs in terms of an "issue," a difficulty, a responsibility, a duty, a chore—almost anything but a source of enjoyment.

To change this stance, parents must do more than make a

general resolution to enjoy themselves with their teenagers. These kinds of general resolutions usually get lost very rapidly in the shuffle of everyday life. Therefore, parents and teenagers have to plan together specific activities that both of them genuinely enjoy and that they can share together. This means sitting down with your teenager and talking honestly about what both of you enjoy doing, deciding how and when you'll do it, and making sure that you actually follow up with your decision. Furthermore, you have to do things together just for the sake of enjoyment on a more or less regular basis, not just as something highly unusual, extra special, or unique. It has to become part of your way of life together to shake loose from a solely problem-oriented focus in your relationship. When you achieve this shift, when you integrate within your everyday pattern of life activities with your adolescent that both of you can share and enjoy, you not only gain the intrinsic pleasure of the activity itself but also strengthen your relationship with each other.

Share activities with your adolescent that both of you genuinely enjoy. Make this a regular part of your lives together.

The key words are *share* and *enjoy*. The adolescent who earns spending money while working for a parent on a Saturday afternoon with the parent in close supervision isn't sharing or necessarily enjoying the experience. The adolescent who sits with the family watching the same television show isn't relating to the other members of the family. The sharing of an activity and interest must be free from the constraints of usual routines and, oftentimes, the familiar home environment. Meeting at the dinner table, perhaps reviewing the day's problems and concerns, having discussions about homework, dates, music lessons, smoking, sex, or any of a variety of other topics won't always permit the carefree abandon of sharing for nothing more than pure pleasure.

Parents fall into the role of advice giver, sounding board, or just plain listener. This kind of give-and-take has value, but the shared moments of enjoyment that were character- istic of earlier years may still be missing.

We found ourselves at one point wrapped up in our par- enting function with the deadly seriousness of psychologists determined to do a better than perfect job of understanding our son, who was sixteen at the time. We listened; we ad- vised; we had long talks about what was going on in his life; we were helpful. There was a purpose to the conversations. The time together always seemed to revolve around some sort of problem.

In an effort to break the pattern at the end of one sum- mer, we decided to take a family bicycle trip. Within a few days we acquired a new perspective about our son. His abili- ty to repair bicycles, make decisions about routes, help plan the trip were impressive. We began to rely on him. Away from home, from familiar settings, his behavior was quite different, and we were struck by his maturity. The emotional tone of our relationship shifted. Instead of heavy-handed weightiness in our discussions, we were able to relate just for fun. Of course, the activity you share with your adolescent need not be anything as major as a bicycle trip. It might simply involve going to the movies together, playing a game both of your enjoy, having a picnic, going to a basketball game. The important point is having fun together.

All of us fall into set ways of responding and behaving in familiar environments. We get enmeshed in our routines; we have patterns of reacting. Escaping into a new situation with one's adolescent is undoubtedly one of the best ways to gain some perspective about each other's behavior and habits.

When we have suggested to parents that they ought to do things with their adolescent just for sheer enjoyment, some parents respond by saying that their teenagers don't want to do anything with them. According to these parents, their adolescents prefer spending time with their friends, and when their parents propose some activity, they either refuse or comply begrudgingly—thus taking the enjoyment out of whatever is done together.

To a certain extent, this kind of response is probably characteristic of many teenagers. After all, for the adolescent, the peer group is of prime importance. But parents must be careful not to use this as an excuse to avoid getting involved with their teenager in a mutually enjoyable activity. When you suggest to your adolescent that you would like to do something together, don't expect to be greeted immediately by unequivocal enthusiasm. If you haven't been engaged regularly in some activities together, it is not unreasonable for the adolescent to be a bit reluctant to jump in enthusiastically without really knowing why you are trying to change your pattern of interaction. So go slowly in making the shift; don't push it. And be absolutely honest about it. Explain why you are making the suggestion, and when the two of you talk about what you might do, make sure the activities you choose are genuinely enjoyable to *both* of you.

Although the entire family can pleasurably share activities together, we also emphasize the crucial importance of one parent and one adolescent getting together and doing something without others in the family. The time spent doesn't have to be lengthy—perhaps as little as a few hours. But being together without the distractions of other people, having the opportunity to share an enjoyable experience just involving the two of you is what really counts. It may take some time to get your adolescent involved, but when you do, you'll find it is well worth whatever effort you have made.

Guidelines for Rational Parenting

Plan your activities together. Make your activities a joint effort right from the beginning so that you can truly share the enjoyment.

If you haven't been involved in pleasurable activities on a regular basis with your teenager before, go slowly; don't push. But make whatever effort it takes to get both of you involved in some enjoyment you can share.

Don't make up artificial activities in which you just go through the motions of "having fun." Be sure that both of you honestly get a kick out of what you're doing.

No Bed of Roses

Help your adolescent learn that some frustration, some tension, anger, and disappointment are normal, natural, and to be expected.

When talking about various methods of child rearing, parents often express a good deal of concern about frustrating their children. They worry about the emotional consequences of frustration and fear that early frustration can lead to later neuroses.

Concern about frustrating a child probably stems from certain psychological theories that have highlighted frustration as the villain in neurotic development. Indeed, there have been countless clinical observations that have identified various kinds of frustration as a source of later emotional difficulties, and thus educators and parents have tried to develop methods of educating and rearing children that protect the child from frustration.

But these efforts have never achieved much success. No matter what we do as teachers or parents, frustration remains one of the stubborn facts of life that no one can escape. No child-rearing practice can entirely prevent a child from being frustrated. Learning to walk, learning to tie shoelaces, learning to read, learning to get along with others—in short, learning almost anything in life—is bound to involve some frustration. Therefore, regardless of parental or educational efforts in this direction, no school and no home can be frustration free.

Although we believe that early and severe frustration can

result in emotional problems later on, we have also seen many cases in which the psychological difficulties an adolescent is going through stem partly from parents' attempts to overprotect their children. These overprotected adolescents have not learned to expect some frustration in the normal course of everyday life. As a result, when they are frustrated outside of the hothouse environment of school or family, they are caught unprepared; they feel that the frustration is abnormal; and they believe that something is wrong either with the world or with themselves. This reaction, in turn, adds to the feelings of self-doubt every normal adolescent experiences.

Help your adolescent learn that life is no bed of roses, that frustration is a normal and inevitable part of living.

Parents' efforts to guard their adolescents from frustration are without doubt motivated by genuine feelings of love and caring. In the long run, however, these efforts do more harm than good. Teenagers growing up in an overprotective environment acquire an unrealistic view of the world and develop expectations of uninterrupted success that can never be fulfilled. They are ill prepared to deal with their own feelings when frustrated, feelings that may be quite normal but can lead to further problems unless these feelings are appropriately channeled and expressed.

The central issue in rational parenting is not frustration itself, but rather the individual's *reaction* to the experience of being frustrated. Emotional disorders do not stem directly from the usual frustrations of daily life, but from the inability to react adequately to whatever frustrations are encountered.

As children mature, as they develop into adolescence, their capacities to respond to stress increase enormously.

However, these capacities must be exercised in order to grow and develop normally so that the adolescent is realistically prepared for adult life. It is crucial, therefore, that within the relative safety of the family and the school adolescents experience realistic frustrations, which will provide opportunities to learn how to respond effectively and appropriately to being frustrated.

This certainly does not mean that parents or teachers should go out of their way to arbitrarily frustrate adolescents with whom they live and work. That, of course, would be absurd. However, it *does* mean that rational parents do not go out of their way to protect adolescents from the normal range of frustrations that everyone meets from time to time.

All of us must live within certain social limits of behavior that require frustrating some of our wishes and desires. All of us must accept certain demands of discipline that involve frustrating immediate gratification of our needs. All of us have some goals that we fail to reach, some hopes that are not fulfilled. These frustrating experiences are all part of the normal day-to-day world of human existence. Meeting frustrating situations or experiences are as inevitable in adolescence as they are a predictable part of adult life. We don't have to create artificial situations for adolescents in order to provide them with learning experiences. At some time every adolescent will run headlong into a frustrating situation, whether it is the failure to make a varsity team, a low grade, not being invited to a party, rejection from a friend, or being handed a cold slice of pizza on a rainy day.

Rational parenting, however, involves more than not overprotecting your adolescent. In a variety of ways a parent should convey the attitude that a certain amount of frustration is normal and to be expected. Probably the most meaningful way of communicating this attitude is through your own reaction to your adolescent's experience of frustration. By all means, the experience should be treated seriously and sympathetically, but at the same time, without viewing the frustration as an unusual, special problem that requires some sort of emergency measure. When your adolescent runs into a frustrating problem, the way you react tells the adolescent a great deal about how much confidence you have in him or her. The rational parent at this point is willing to take a chance on the adolescent's growing maturity.

If parents successfully communicate the message that being frustrated is part of everyday living, their adolescents learn that experiencing frustration is not abnormal, in fact not particularly unusual; and they gain added confidence from the reaization that when they are frustrated, there is probably nothing especially wrong with the world or with themselves. Thus, they learn to live with one of the basic facts of life.

In addition to helping their adolescents learn that some frustration is a normal part of living, rational parents can also help their adolescents learn to accept and deal with the emotional reactions associated with being frustrated. This is especially important with regard to feelings of anger that are commonly evoked by frustration. All of us in the process of growing up must learn how to handle our anger. At two years old the frustrated child may kick and scream, and while parents may not be very happy with their child's emotional outburst, they probably tolerate it because, after all, the two-year-old is "only a child." The situation is quite different for an eighteen-year-old. Kicking and screaming in response to frustration is not likely to be tolerated because, after all, the eighteen-year-old is "nearly an adult."

As adults we are expected to control and channel our

anger; this is part of being a civilized human being. But this doesn't mean that frustrated adults don't feel as intensely angry as any two-year-old child might feel. The chief difference is in the behavior, not in the strength of the feelings evoked.

Anger is a major source of psychological problems in our society. Some children learn very early that feeling angry is "bad" and even dangerous because it is liable to lead to punishment. As a result, they try desperately to inhibit any feelings of anger, striving to be "nice," and when they fail to control their angry feelings, they become tense and guilty. Trying to live totally free of angry feelings is rarely, if ever, successful—or possible. These feelings can be inhibited, repressed, pushed out of consciousness so that the individual is not even aware of his or her own emotions. But the anger doesn't disappear. It smolders, causes greater and greater tension and guilt, and eventually is expressed in neurotic symptoms or sometimes in violent, explosive outbursts.

At the other extreme are those who never learn to control their angry, aggressive behavior, those who remain, in this respect, two-year-olds throughout life. They escape the tension and guilt of inhibited, repressed hostility, but they, too, inevitably create their own psychological difficulties. Their hostile behavior generates counter-hostility in others. When they are frustrated and respond aggressively, attacking and hurting others, their behavior evokes anger, aggression, and attacks from others. They live in a vicious circle of hostility and counter-hostility, and they become increasingly fearful and anxious.

This was precisely the kind of difficulty Melissa was caught in when she was referred to the guidance counselor at her school. Her home room teacher reported that fifteen-year-old Melissa displayed temper tantrums when stressed. An appealing girl, she was friendly and responsive to her teachers and competent in her school work. However, when she encountered the slightest frustration, such as the pressure of an extra assignment or the threat of an unexpected test, she reacted with tantrums. Melissa lashed out at her teachers, used profanity, threw her books on the floor and "exploded."

At the recommendation of the school, Melissa was given a thorough medical examination. There was nothing physically wrong. She was a well-developed, well-coordinated fifteen-year-old, above average in intelligence.

In talking about the problem with us, Melissa's mother said, "I made up my mind that with my kids I wasn't going to raise them how I was raised." She described her own childhood, which had been characterized by severe home discipline. "You got up from the table before my father said you could and that was the end. You got a good crack on the backside. My father and my mother both had us kids toe the line. You bet your life we didn't talk back or fight."

So with her own children, Melissa's mother bent over backwards to be permissive. The children, Melissa and her sister and brother, were encouraged to "let off steam." If the youngsters were angry at each other, they were free to express that anger in any way, whether it meant shouting, fighting physically, or even talking back to their parents. "I know they don't mean what they say. It's best they get what's on their minds out where it belongs. I know what it means to stay bottled up with your feelings."

As a result of her mother's overconcern about her daughter being frustrated, Melissa had never learned appropriate external limits. For her, anger was to be expressed directly; frustration to be handled by explosive behavior. In an effort to raise her daughter to be a "free spirit," Melissa's mother allowed the extreme, and at fifteen Melissa found herself in trouble at school. Her codes of behavior were acceptable in her own home, but in the larger world she was entering these codes were not acceptable and could not be tolerated.

Let your adolescent know that feeling angry when frustrated is a normal human reaction and certainly nothing to feel ashamed or guilty about. Focus your adolescent's attention on learning how to handle angry feelings without repressing them or without exploding in childish ways.

Adolescents are especially sensitive to frustration, and they're prone to being frustrated. In the course of trying out new interests, expanding their range of activities as part of growing up, they are bound to be frustrated from time to time, and the sense of frustration is often intensified by an underlying lack of self-confidence that many teenagers feel. Furthermore, anger in response to frustration is not at all unusual in the lives of adolescents, and it is crucial that they learn how to deal with these feelings.

A first step in learning to handle their anger is understanding that feeling angry when frustrated is a normal and natural reaction. There is nothing wrong or abnormal about becoming angry; everyone experiences this emotional reaction, and there is no rational reason for being ashamed of being angry, feeling guilty, or trying to inhibit or repress the feelings. The capacity to become angry is part of everyone's human heritage, and when adolescents fully understand and appreciate this fact, they will be neither surprised nor particularly disturbed by their own experiences of anger.

Rational parents help their adolescents achieve this understanding by explicitly recognizing their adolescents' feelings and unequivocally communicating the message that feeling anger is perfectly normal and, given the circumstances of frustration, to be expected. From a psychological point of view, the problem with anger is not the feeling itself, but rather what is done about the feeling. Neither repressing anger nor expressing it in uncontrolled outbursts of aggression work very effectively. Eventually, both styles of response lead to psychological trouble. Therefore, adolescents have to learn how to express their anger in socially acceptable, mature ways.

In our society, by far the most common way adults express anger is verbally—by talking—and there are certain unwritten rules that govern angry speech. For example, at a football game it might be acceptable for fans to express their angry disagreement with a referee's decision by some loud shouting; in a classroom, the same kind of angry expression in reaction to a teacher's decision is likely to elicit not only surprise but also some punishment. In a social situation it might be appropriate to express anger by sarcastic humor, while in a more formal work situation the same kind of sarcastic humor may be viewed as highly inappropriate. If two teenagers are working together and one thoughtlessly frustrates the other, the frustrated and angry teenager might appropriately express the anger verbally without beating around the bush. In contrast, if the same teenager has a job and is working with a boss who carelessly causes some frustration, the same degree of anger might be felt but a more indirect form of expression, such as complaining to a friend, would probably be much more appropriate.

We cannot specify all the unspoken rules that govern acceptable ways of expressing anger in our culture. They differ somewhat from situation to situation and from one subculture to another. The important point, however, is that in order to get along in society without becoming overly tense, inhibited, and neurotic, a person must learn how to express anger in socially acceptable ways.

This learning doesn't begin in adolescence. Very early in life young children start learning the dos and don'ts of their society. But this learning becomes even more important during adolescence partly because frustration and anger are more frequent at this stage of life and partly because the capacity to handle one's anger is an important step toward maturity.

The most important role parents play in this learning process is as models in dealing with their own emotional reactions. If a parent responds to frustration with a temper tantrum, it is not surprising that his or her teenager behaves in the same way.

We recall one man who talked with us about his son's impossible temper. He described how this sixteen-year-old reacted to frustration by shouting, slamming his bedroom door, pounding tables, and occasionally breaking objects. His son's behavior infuriated him. He considered such actions infantile. The explosions had a volcanic-like style, he reported. His son would be speaking in a normal voice and then the intensity and volume would increase and then "he stands there bellowing. He doesn't even seem to be aware he's shouting. There isn't any controlling him when he gets like that."

The father got up out of the chair and leaned his hands on the desk. "I feel like grabbing him by the collar or throwing water in his face to cool him down. He may be sixteen . . . "—at this point the father raised a clenched fist and pounded on the desk—"but he acts like a two-year-old at times." A framed picture fell and glass fragments scattered on the floor. It was all right, we assured him; the glass could be easily replaced. More importantly, the point had been made; the son was merely doing a very good job of imitating his father's temper tantrums.

In addition to serving as models of appropriate behavior, rational parents are clear and firm about limits in expressing anger. A rational parent must convey the message that while it is perfectly all right to feel angry and to express it, there are certain behaviors that are acceptable and other behaviors that will not be tolerated.

At one stage during our children's adolescence, they typically released their anger through a stream of four-letter words accompanied by table banging, door slamming, or some other physical explosiveness. The damage done by their physical explosions was minimal, but the stream of four-letter words became an increasingly greater source of irritation. We know that our dislike of profanity stems from our own childhoods. We recall our mouths being washed out with soap the first time "damn" was uttered. In trying to be "With it," we had bent over backwards to accept the modern lingo, and at the same time we resented it. One day, when the front door was slammed, breaking glass in a storm window, and a five-minute monologue of four-letter words followed, our tolerance level reached the breaking point.

We were furious, and yet the fault was as much ours as the adolescents involved. We hadn't made the ground rules explicit, and we realized then that we should clearly set the limits of acceptable behavior. It was okay for either boy to get angry. They certainly met situations that angered them. However, we had had enough of swearing. We had had enough of tables being pounded and doors being slammed. They could run around the block to let off steam. They could go bash a tennis ball against a wall. We would listen to anything they had to say, but just as we wouldn't shout obscenities at them, we in turn didn't want them to swear at us.

We may be old-fashioned, we may be dated, but these were our conditions. "How would you like it if we call you a f-----b-----?" we asked them. After their initial shock at hearing us utter these words, they agreed that they wouldn't like it very much.

We didn't curtail their anger or their expression of it. However, we insisted that the mode of expression be changed. We had been as much at fault as our children in our efforts to be modern parents, to bend over backwards to make sure they "let it all hang out." But we realized that we had to be consistent with our values, and we couldn't adjust that swiftly. In trying to overcome the generation gap of language, we were becoming more and more irritated and less and less helpful in our relationships with our adolescents.

No one can tell a parent what behaviors are acceptable. Parents must decide themselves what they will tolerate and what they won't. And once they decide, they must then make the limits very clear to their teenagers. Parents must also be thoroughly consistent in their own behavior as well as in the expectations they communicate to their adolescents. Without this kind of clarity, firmness, and consistency of limits and expectations, we cannot expect adolescents to learn how to handle their angry feelings in reasonable and socially acceptable ways.

Guidelines for Rational Parenting
Don't try to overprotect your teenager from the potential frustrations of the real world. Remember that the home and family provide a relatively safe environment in which the adolescent can learn how to react to being frustrated. The way an adolescent will deal with frustrations met later on in the outside world will partly depend upon how that

adolescent has learned to respond to problems within the family situation.

When your adolescent is frustrated, in most instances the most important thing you can do is convey the message that you have confidence in your adolescent being able to handle the problem in his or her own way. Offer whatever practical help might be necessary, but don't take over the problem solving.

When your adolescent reacts to frustration with anger, recognize these feelings as normal and legitimate. You can say, "It's okay to feel angry. What's important is how you deal with it."

Be clear in your own mind about acceptable ways of expressing anger, and then make sure your adolescent knows your views. Is it all right to swear? To yell and scream? To pound the wall? What are the limits you can tolerate? No one else can tell you what limits are right for you; you have to think through this issue yourself.

Once you've decided, make sure your adolescent knows what these limits are, and stick to them. They are *your* views, the limits *you* can tolerate, the ways of expressing anger that *you* can live with. The best time to talk to your adolescent about acceptable ways of dealing with anger is when neither of you is angry. Yelling about limits when your adolescent is in the middle of an outburst of temper will probably only fan the flames of anger. So, talk to your adolescent about what is and is not acceptable to you.

On Being an Individual

Encourage and support your adolescent's right to be an individual, different from others.

All of us live in a network of interdependencies. We depend on others, and others in turn depend on us. That's part of everyday life for everyone. But teenagers are especially dependent upon their peers. They are striving to break away from the childhood patterns of relying on their parents, and in this process of growing out of one kind of dependency, they need the support of others who are facing the same developmental hurdles. Thus, the network of interdependencies among teenagers becomes strengthened as a normal consequence of the changes that occur in the relationships between adolescents and their parents.

At the same time, adolescents are also striving to establish their own unique identities, to realize their particular talents, tastes, values, goals, desires—in short, to become individuals in their own right. This drive for individuality becomes an increasingly powerful source of motivation. It results in tension between the movement towards independence and the countermovement of dependence on others; between the need for individuality, for inner direction, and the need to belong, to be supported psychologically by others. We recall in detail an incident in our own community. At the time, tennis wasn't as popular as it is today. Many of the adolescent boys in town viewed tennis as a sport for oddballs and weaklings. Football, baseball, and basketball were the only *manly* activities worth pursuing.

One afternoon our son, fourteen years old at the time, met us at the tennis courts. His shirt was ripped, tennis racket twisted out of shape, and his bicycle tires punctured.

"What happened to you?"

"A fight."

"Where?"

"At the Corner Store."

"Why?"

"Guys from town—six, maybe more."

"Do you know them?"

"Some."

"How old were they?"

"I dunno—same as me—maybe one younger. I think one was older."

"How did it start?"

"I came by on my bicycle. I was going to get candy. They started at me."

"You didn't say anything to them?"

"No—they said something about kids who wear white tennis shorts. And they tried to grab my racket. That's how my shirt got torn. One pulled my shirt. They're on the baseball teams in the town league. They don't like tennis."

"That's obvious," we replied. "But why did they fight with you?" This attack didn't make sense to us. Why fight with a boy for doing something that wasn't their concern?

"One told me he didn't like the way my tennis whites looked. He said he'd fix them. That's how the gum got on my shorts. He put bubble gum on while I was fighting with the others. My racket is broken."

We sat on a bench near the courts struggling to understand their behavior.

"Why didn't you get me started in Little League?" our son asked.

"You weren't interested," we told him.

"How did you know?"

"You said you liked tennis."

"*You* liked tennis," he told us. "You people pushed me into tennis. *You* were the ones who said, 'Let's play tennis' and dragged me to the courts."

"We never made you come. You could have played baseball."

"I thought you wanted me to. That's the reason I came. The other kids went out for baseball. It would be a lot better if I played baseball."

"How?" we asked. "So those kids could be your friends? You want those boys as friends?"

"Why not? What's wrong? No one around here plays tennis—just me. Sure I like tennis. So what? Maybe I'd like baseball the same—not those kids, but there are others. They wouldn't think I was different."

"Is that what you want—to play baseball?"

"I don't know what I want," he told us.

From an early age he had been encouraged in many aspects of life to do his own thing, follow his own direction and not the group's. All sorts of maxims we had learned in our childhoods were passed on to our son: "He who walks alone walks furthest." "Be the master of yourself—don't bend like a willow to the group demands." "What would you do if everyone in a group jumped off a cliff—would you jump too?"

All of these aphorisms seemed to have worked when our son was small and ran into situations in which he chose to follow his own direction rather than conform to his peers. However, at this moment, the sayings seemed to mock us. Our despondent son, sitting with a broken racket, after a senseless fight, was resentful. There didn't seem to be too much in the way of rewards for walking alone. It also wasn't very comforting at the time to reassure him that in the long run he was going to be a lot better off for not having followed the dictates of the group, to have had the courage to be independent. Visions of future comforts aren't very soothing at the moment of crisis.

There is one postscript to the story. Years later, after tennis had become the "in" thing to do in our town, our son, now an adult, was reminded of this early experience in his life. One afternoon on a visit home he went out to the courts. Two of the boys who had been involved in the fight years before were playing. They had just taken up the game and when they saw our son, they invited him to play, asking if he would give them some help with their game.

"I remember you used to play a lot of tennis," one boy told him. "You never went out for baseball." No one mentioned anything about the fight.

This conflict about inner- and other-directedness is one of the central psychological issues of our culture, and it is during adolescence that each of us experiences this conflict in an especially compelling form. There is probably no other stage of life when the need for peer support, the need to belong to a group outside of the family, is stronger. Teenagers are not only breaking ties with their parents; they are also trying out new roles, facing new demands from the environment, and experiencing dramatic changes physically as well as psychologically. This stage of life is normally full of trial and error, with the emphasis sometimes on error, and there's bound to be a good deal of stress, tension and anxiety. Only the rare teenager avoids suffering some loss in self-confidence during these years of development, despite the superficial displays of bravado we see in this age group. The need for some sort of reassurance from others, the need for social acceptance and social approval is greater than ever before. Parental acceptance and approval at this stage is not enough. Teenagers need the acceptance, the reassurance, and the approval of their peers.

Don't fight against the teenager's need to be accepted and approved by peers. Remember that the adolescent's desire to be part of a group is a normal part of growing up.

But there is a price paid for peer support, the price of conformity. To be accepted by a group demands some degree of conformity to group norms—using the same kind of language, dressing in similar styles, sharing the same beliefs, tastes, and values. This phenomenon is readily observable among almost any group of teenage friends. Everyone in the group may listen to the same music, buy the same records, prefer the same musicians. Their style of dress may be so similar to one another that they might as well be wearing a uniform. They probably use the same slang, the same special language that stamps them as group members, and they often share the same attitudes and stereotypes, particularly about those who are not members of their group.

Adults sometimes think of adolescents as a single group; we speak of "the teenage culture" as if all adolescents shared the same kinds of beliefs and behaviors. There are in fact a variety of "teenage cultures" reflecting quite different attitudes and styles of behavior; but in each case, to be a member of a group and to receive the psychological support of the group, there is an implicit, usually unspoken but powerful demand to conform to the group's norms.

Although a great deal of attention has been focused on the adolescent's drive to gain independence from parents, by middle-to-late adolescence perhaps an even more profound psychological problem stems from the tension between the

need to gain a sense of individuality and the need to conform to peer group norms. If this conflict is not resolved in
adolescence, it may remain a long-term source of tension.
For the sake of being accepted by others, adolescents may
distort their own organic experience. They may adopt interests, values, and behaviors that are incongruent with their
own inner-directed impulses towards self-realization, and as
a result their development as individuals may be warped or
stunted.

Fighting against a teenager's need to be accepted by peers
is usually a fruitless battle that often results in strengthening
the adolescent's ties to a group rather than weakening them.
This occurred with Richard, the son of wealthy parents, who
became involved with a radical political group. As his interest in the group and its activities increased, his parents
stepped up their hostility and critical disapproval. Forced to
be on the defensive, Richard intensified his involvement.

The family had always been active in community affairs
and discussed social issues at home, but their son's taking
this interest to an extreme was something they hadn't
bargained for. Richard's father agreed that social change,
social movements, had their place, but he maintained that
changes had to occur within the existing framework of the
democratic process. He resented the fact that young revo-
lutionaries were ready to upset his world. When his son
brought home pamphlets describing exploitation of under-
developed nations by huge corporations (including one in
which his father held a high position), the pamphlets were
dismissed as trash, written by "empty-headed, disturbed
kids."

At times his father attempted to argue logically with
Richard. He agreed that changes were needed in the society;
however, in his opinion, youngsters in these groups were

hardly equipped with the expertise needed to make such changes possible. The group of youngsters who met several times a week were dismissed as a "bunch of middle-class do-gooders who didn't know what they were talking about."

Richard countered by saying that people in the group weren't playing games and they weren't talkers. He told his father that several of the group had spent the summer harvesting crops and encouraging the members to unionize. Richard was the one member of the group with a regular allowance, and he began using his money to pay for food and drinks served at the meetings. Richard's mother felt that Richard's acceptance into the group was because of his money. "They are using him. My son doesn't know what is really going on. He never showed much interest in politics before. And he doesn't have the facts to back up what he says."

Each time Richard attended a meeting, his father challenged him on what had occurred. His mother pointed out that other than at meetings, the boys in the radical group had nothing to do with him. "They never call you up. They never ask you to go anywhere. Can't you see that it's your money—our money—they want? If they were really friends, the friendship would extend outside of these meetings."

Richard argued that this wasn't the case. They were friends because of their similar interests. He pointed out that at first he had only been invited to group meetings, but recently the leaders (boys somewhat older) had invited him to attend the planning committee sessions. He insisted that they appreciated his ideas and respected him.

Until Richard had taken up with the radical group, he had been involved with music and history. An avid reader and clarinetist, he had had little time for group activities until a chance invitation to a meeting of the radical group. The boy who invited him to join had been someone Richard looked up to in school. Somewhat older, this boy had been politically active in school groups, and Richard had felt flattered when asked to come along to a meeting. The boy graduated from high school and went away to college. Richard, still in his junior year, remained with the group.

Both parents were determined to get Richard to cut loose from the radical group. Richard's parents viewed his friends as troublemakers primarily because of the radical political philosophy the group so vocally espoused. Seeing their son "hooked up with a bunch of irresponsible kids" was frightening and disturbing. Family conversations were dominated by disparaging remarks about the boys.

The parents' efforts to get Richard to break away from the group had exactly the opposite result. As his parents attacked his friends, Richard became more and more defensive, and the arguments merely led to Richard becoming even closer than before to the group his parents were worried about.

Parents must remember that their adolescents really need the support of their friends, so parental attempts to break up these relationships are almost always bound to fail and frequently cause a great deal of family tension. However, while parents must respect and appreciate their adolescent's need to be part of a group, they should also encourage and support their adolescent's right to be different. Without lecturing, without nagging, without making it a major emotional issue in the family, parents should get across the message that while everyone needs the acceptance and support of others, we also need the opportunity to be ourselves. This doesn't mean fighting the group, being different just to be different, going against the norms of a group merely to rebel. But it does mean that adolescents must have a chance to discover their own internal directions, to become aware of their inner-directed impulses, and to trust their own sense of values. They must learn to make choices and judgments independent of others and to develop their own potentials as unique individuals.

When your adolescent is in conflict between conforming to a group and fulfilling his or her own individuality, don't try to minimize the stress your adolescent might feel about being different from friends. But show that you trust your teenager's judgment and have faith in your teenager's personal strength to become a genuinely inner-directed individual.

Parents can foster their adolescent's individuality by paying attention to their teenager's inner-directed interests, by encouraging their teenager to explore and discover his or her own values, and by accepting and reinforcing their teenager's efforts to become independent.

The importance of parents' respect for an adolescent's individuality was underscored for us by the comments of a young musician who described how much his parents' respect meant to him when he was growing up. Joseph recalled the conflict he felt as a child between his music and the activities of the other kids in his neighborhood. "They were out playing football. I was in playing the cello."

It hadn't been easy to divide his world. There were times when he bitterly resented practicing. There were times when the taunts of his classmates became oppressive. Because of his personal dedication, he had fewer of the usual kinds of social interactions or informal relationships during childhood and adolescence. He told us that until he went away to school at eighteen, his life had been an island of isolation. There were some advantages, of course—the rewards from his family and teachers, youth concerts in which he starred.

But there were disadvantages, too—the loneliness he often felt, the desire to belong, and the imagined picture of how much fun everyone but he was having after school. The picture changed, he said, when he left home and went to a music school, where he discovered other young people who had been similarly encouraged. "I don't think I could have reached this point without the kind of early training I had. It's a decision I suppose kids have to make. But they don't really make it alone. I think the parents really make the decision which starts a career like mine."

He doesn't regret the past. He feels he knows who he is and what he can do with his talent. He told us there probably always has to be a choice when you're growing up. "You have to put off the kinds of pleasures most teenagers have, and wait until later." Now that he has found groups of people like himself he isn't sorry about those years. "Going off alone is hard, but if I hadn't gone off alone as I did, I don't think I ever would have acquired the skills in music I have. It's a price I paid, not being part of a group."

Joseph's parents helped Joseph face himself and recognize that in some important respects he was different from his friends. Partly as a result of this parental support and encouragement, Joseph was able to develop in a way that genuinely fulfilled his individual talents—to become a person who is authentically himself. There is nothing more important that parents can help their teenagers achieve.

Pay attention to your adolescent's efforts to develop a personal sense of values, and be sure that you clearly show respect for these values, even though they may be different from yours.

Pursuing one's own inner-directed path isn't always easy, especially for adolescents. Because of their need for the acceptance and approval of other adolescents, being different can sometimes be a threatening and stressful experience. Parents can't "talk away" the stress their teenagers might feel, and it does no good to make believe that the stress isn't real. But parents can help by letting their teenagers know that they understand and appreciate that going their own way, regardless of what their friends say and do, can sometimes be very rough. And at the same time parents must convey a sense of trust in their teenager's judgment, the belief that their teenager has the personal strength to see the tough times through. A good deal of one's personal strength depends upon the faith others have in us. If teenagers know that their parents have faith in them as individuals, they are much more likely to develop the self-confidence necessary for healthy psychological growth.

Every adolescent is a unique individual, different from everyone else. Therefore, in considering what we can do to help our adolescents become individuals in their own right, we are dealing with an issue that all parents and adolescents must face. Our goal as parents should be to help our adolescents discover their own individuality and develop the personal strength needed to resist the pressures of group conformity. If parents can achieve this goal, and can learn to respect and appreciate their adolescents' individuality, they will have given their teenagers one of the most valuable gifts any person can give another—the opportunity to genuinely become one's own self.

Guidelines for Rational Parenting

Remember that an adolescent's first step in gaining a sense of individuality depends upon becoming independent from parents. Part of the process of an adolescent becoming independent involves disagreeing with parents. Sometimes parents don't understand why their adolescent disagrees with them. Their adolescent's opinions may not make logical sense and may even seem detrimental to his or her own interests. But the rational parent recognizes that the process of disagreeing with parents is often an important step in the adolescent's growing individuation. Even if their teenager's views don't make logical sense, they almost always make psycho-logical sense. Stick to your own views if you believe they are right for you, but listen to your adolescent's opinions without prejudging them. Agree to disagree, and appreciate these disagreements as important evidence that your adolescent is becoming an individual in his or her own right.

Actively encourage your adolescent to do things on his or her own. If you do, your adolescent will realize that you are willing to take a risk on his or her growing maturity and that you honestly value his or her independence. Whenever you have the opportunity, foster this maturity by encouraging and reinforcing independence.

Resolving Conflicts

When a conflict develops between you and your adolescent, stop blaming, start understanding, and above all keep talking to each other.

When conflicts develop between parents and adolescents, sometimes both parent and adolescent spend a great deal of time, energy, and ingenuity building a case against each other. When we, as psychologists, get involved, our first exposure to the problem is often a series of accusations that sound like the arguments of two prosecuting attorneys. A parent may set out to prove that the teenager is lazy, irresponsible, thoughtless, and entirely to blame for whatever problem has arisen. In rebuttal, the adolescent may be equally eloquent in establishing that the parent is insensitive, unfair, narrow-minded, old-fashioned and unable to understand either the teenager or the teenager's world. The arguments go around and around, each person concerned primarily with assigning blame to the other, and each one so wrapped up in his or her own arguments that the other person is rarely heard—much less understood.

The basic difficulty in these arguments is that the aim of both parent and adolescent—assigning blame to the other person—is largely irrelevant to solving whatever problem has arisen. As long as that mutual aim remains, little can be accomplished.

To short-circuit this vicious cycle of blame and counter-blame, one person needs to realize that whenever there is a problem between two people—between parent and adolescent, husband and wife, friends, co-workers, or any other two people—*both* inevitably contribute to the difficulties in their relationship. Between parent and adolescent, it is never really a matter of one being selfish or lazy, insensitive or unfair, and the other being perfect. Both parent and adolescent contribute their share to whatever difficulties develop between them, and the sooner they stop playing the blame game with each other, the sooner they can change the direction towards mutual understanding and eventual resolution of their troubles.

When disagreements arise between you and your adolescent, don't get caught in the trap of assigning blame. Remember that you are a parent, not a prosecuting attorney, and that nothing gets resolved by proving your adolescent guilty.

In our experience, the parent usually recognizes this point most readily, not because he or she is older or wiser, but rather because the parent in these arguments usually has the more secure position, greater power, and is under less immediate strain. This is not to say that parents react any less emotionally than adolescents do in these situations, but after the accusations, the threats and counter-threats, it is the parent who usually can shift more readily from attack and defense to communicating and understanding. And with this shift in focus, the interaction between parent and adolescent can move from assigning blame to gaining mutual understanding.

Although running arguments between parent and adolescent are unquestionably irritating and sometimes emotionally explosive, they are nowhere near as serious a problem as total blocks in communication. As long as parent and adolescent keep on talking to each other, even if the talk is mostly fighting, there is a chance of breaking through to some reasonable solution. A fight can be painful, but at least when parent and adolescent are fighting, they are in some sort of contact with each other. A much more devastating problem occurs when parent and adolescent withdraw from each other, and communication breaks down altogether.

This was the point Janice and her father reached after a series of verbal battles regarding her social behavior. Communication had come to a standstill.

"He doesn't know I'm not talking to him," she told us. "He thinks because I say hello, goodnight and that sort of thing I'm not really mad. To me that's not talking."

Not only was she refusing to speak to him, but she went to great lengths to avoid being in his presence. "If he comes into the living room to watch TV and I'm sitting there, I get up and say something like 'I have to do homework.' He hasn't caught on yet that I'm not going to have much to do with him."

Difficulties began when Janice's father discovered one of his daughter's boyfriends lounging on her bed.

Janice said that she was sitting on the floor, sorting records. Her boyfriend was stretched out on her bed. "What was so wrong? He told the boy he didn't want him near me again. He made us both out to be pretty terrible—the boy even worse than me. He said it was the boy's fault. Fault for what?

"The door was half open. There was no reason for him to act like that. I felt awful. All we were doing was listening to records."

After the young man left, Janice's father lectured to her for "hours." He told her he was hurt, disappointed, fearful about what would happen to her. "He told me I couldn't go out anymore. I told him he wouldn't stop me. He wouldn't come right out and say it, but he hinted that we were having sex. 'In the bedroom with the door open?' I asked him. That would be dumb. He said I couldn't bring boys up to my room, like sex couldn't take place anywhere but in my room if that was what I was going to do. He wouldn't even listen to me. Even when he cooled off, he wouldn't listen."

Janice resented his behavior during the following weeks. "He spied on me. It was like I was two years old. He even picked up the extension telephone to listen to whom I was talking to. I pretended I didn't know who he was, and I said something about people listening on the line."

Part of her father's attempts to control Janice's behavior included long speeches about what was going to happen to her unless she behaved. He recounted stories about daughters of friends of his who had gone astray.

"He never was like that with me before," Janice told us. She and her father had always enjoyed a good relationship. Some of her friends had difficulties with their fathers or mothers. Janice had only positive experiences until she reached dating age.

"The first time I had a date he told the boy I had to be in by 10 p.m. or he wouldn't let me go out again. I thought he was kidding."

Since the bedroom incident Janice has felt that her father has been behaving like a watchdog. He probes into her personal life, checks on where she is going. "Even if it's Saturday afternoon, he'll ask me for details."

What bothered her most was her father's refusal to believe that she and the boy were only listening to records and talking. At first when he brought up the subject, Janice defended herself. "We'd start talking and then end up yelling at each other. I couldn't take it anymore, so I made up my mind not to talk to him more than I had to. At least we wouldn't be screaming at each other."

By the time Janice and her father talked to us, both of them had reached the point where they felt the situation was hopeless. The problem had started with the daughter's striving for independence, which is certainly normal in adolescence, and her father's concern about the possible consequences of Janice's growing independence. It would be meaningless to argue about which one was right and which one was wrong; the important point to recognize is that both of them contributed to the conflict that eventually led to the much more serious problem of a total breakdown in their communication with each other.

Janice's father saw her behavior as potentially dangerous and viewed her refusal to obey as a personal rejection of him. On the other hand, Janice viewed her father as irrationally demanding and restrictive and incapable of understanding her point of view. The way in which each saw the other only served to increase anger and anxiety felt by both of them, and in reaction to these feelings, father and daughter stepped up the level of their attacks and defenses that finally led them into a vicious circle of frustration, anger, and non-communication.

As Janice's father became more demanding, she became more withdrawn and secretive, even about activities that had nothing to do with their initial disagreement. Finally, the situation became so painful for both of them that they withdrew from each other, and communication between them virtually stopped. They lived in sullen silence with each other, feeling angry and distrustful, anxious and depressed, and hopelessly trapped.

During our first meeting with Janice and her parents, it

became clear that the disruption in communication between them was a far more serious problem than the argument that started them on the way to their present dilemma. Each was entrenched in a seemingly unshakable defensive position that prevented them from reaching out to each other, from sharing their thoughts and feelings, and from working out a solution that both could live with. Our primary aim in working with them was to reestablish communication, get them talking to each other again, and provide an opportunity for them to rebuild a relationship that had nearly been shattered.

Using the principles of rational parenting, we helped Janice and her father to begin communicating with each other, at first briefly and hesitantly, but gradually becoming more and more open, less defensive, and with increased understanding. Our first step was to establish a ground rule for their discussions: *Don't prosecute each other.* In their earlier battles they had both been so concerned with building a case against each other that neither had ever really listened to what the other was saying. Instead, we suggested, they should begin by trying to understand the other's point of view.

To achieve this empathetic understanding we asked each one to express his or her own views and feelings as fully as possible and, in doing so, to make sure they used *I-messages* ("I think" or "I feel"). Janice's father talked about his own anxiety about Janice being hurt, and he discussed his opinions of sexual activities among teenagers, recognizing that his personal views stemmed from the values he had developed early in his own life. In addition, he talked about his feeling of being hurt and rejected by Janice as a result of their disagreement. Janice, on the other hand, emphasized her feelings of being hurt by the message of distrust her father conveyed, and she expressed her feelings of frustration in trying to convince her father that she was, in fact, trustworthy.

As each one spoke, we urged the other to listen without interrupting and without preparing a rebuttal. In the beginning, it wasn't easy for either Janice or her father. Both tended to slip into their earlier positions of attack and defense, but each time they started to attack or defend, we reminded them that their aim was to listen in order to understand. After a few meetings together, they were able to catch themselves and thus short-circuit the cycle of miscommunication.

As a consequence of her efforts to sympathize with her father's point of view, Janice gradually came to the realization that her father was not just being nasty, narrow-minded, and unfair, but that he was genuinely concerned about her, though his behavior had failed to convey this concern. She also became aware of her father's feeling of rejection and reported that this was the first time in her life that she realized a parent could feel rejected by a child. On the other hand, Janice's father recognized that she was not fighting him merely because she was hostile and negativistic, but that for Janice the central issue was one of trust. And he realized how his own behavior had communicated the message of distrust.

The disagreements between Janice and her father didn't magically disappear, and from time to time tempers flared, but both father and daughter learned to live with their disagreements and to accept each other's emotional reactions without feeling unduly threatened. Most important, they learned how to keep the communication channels open between them regardless of whatever temporary stresses they might experience. And by virtue of their ability to keep talking to each other without retreating into defensive silence, they were able to strengthen and reinforce the relationship between them. *Above all, keep talking to each other no matter what happens. Retreats into sullen silence can only make matters worse, so be the first to break the silence, and make every effort to keep the communication channels open between you and your adolescent.*

We do not mean to imply that merely talking to each other automatically leads to a resolution of problems that develop between parents and teenagers. Obviously, talk is only a medium for exchanging ideas, opinions, and information, and for sharing feelings, values, and experiences. Through this exchange and sharing, resolutions can be achieved. But talking to each other is a *necessary* condition for this exchange and sharing, a condition of communication between parent and adolescent that makes the solution of their difficulties possible.

A problem we sometimes face with parents stems from what we believe is a false sense of parental prerogative; that is, parents may feel hurt and insulted by comments their teenagers have made in the course of their battles, and as a result, the parents refuse to continue talking until their teenagers apologize, "give in," or in some way demonstrate respect for the parents' status and position. In most cases, apology is the last thing in the teenager's mind, and the situation rapidly deteriorates, with the parent feeling bitter and hurt by the teenager's "disrespect" and the teenager feeling even more frustrated and angry.

In confronting this problem, parents must recognize that it is really *not* a matter of respect or disrespect, and their continued focus on the issue of whether or not their teenagers have shown proper respect for their parents will only make the situation progressively worse rather than better. Adolescents don't attack their parents because of disrespect or even lack of appreciation. Adolescents behave hostilely because they are frustrated, threatened, and often anxious and insecure. Neither parents nor adolescents have a special license to behave with irrational hostility, but when people fight with each other, especially people who are as close emotionally as parents and adolescents, hurtful comments are bound to be made, insults are inevitable, and the limits of normal interpersonal respect are very likely to be transgressed.

Don't focus on the issue of "proper respect," for this is an issue that can very easily get in the way of dealing effectively with the more significant problems that arise in relations between parents and adolescents. Rather, concentrate your efforts on continuing to keep the communication channels between you and your teenagers open. Stop playing the blame game, and strive for a sense of mutual understanding with your adolescents.

Waiting for apologies or for any special signs of respect or appreciation from your teenager is not helpful; just keep on talking, keep sharing, and keep on trying to understand each other. Genuine respect and appreciation will grow out of these efforts and in the long run will be much more meaningful in your relationship with your adolescent than apologies are.

Guidelines for Rational Parenting
When conflicts between you and your adolescent develop, remember:
• Stop the blame game.
• Be the first one to break the vicious cycle of attack and defense by stopping your attacks, making defense unnecessary, and working toward mutual empathetic understanding.

• Through the use of *I-messages*, express your opinions and feelings as clearly as you can. And when your adolescent speaks, listen in order to understand. Pay attention. Don't interrupt. Empathize; don't analyze or judge.

• Stay focused on the immediate conflict. Don't generalize to other issues.

• Recognize that people can disagree and still live together with genuine affection and respect. And be prepared to work out realistic, down-to-earth compromises that both you and your adolescent can live with.

• Don't let conventional, superficial signs of "proper respect" get in the way of your search for mutual understanding.

• Above all, keep the communication channels open.

Rational Parenting in Everyday Life

*Begin with the daily events
of living together.*

Rational parenting means much more than responding to problems or dealing with specific issues in your adolescent's life. It means developing a relationship in which both you and your adolescent can genuinely be yourselves, with a firm sense of independence, and also an acceptance and appreciation of your mutual interdependence. It means a relationship in which together you can honestly and openly express your values, attitudes, and feelings and share your views of the world, all the while maintaining your own individuality. It means listening in order to understand, not only when there is a problem to be solved but in your daily interactions with each other. In short, it means incorporating the process of rational parenting into everyday life.

To achieve this goal, begin with the small, daily events of living together. In the course of your daily conversations, whatever the topic might be, practice sharing your opinions and feelings (expressed as *your* opinions and *your* feelings), but also practice paying close attention, without interrupting, to what your adolescent has to say. Practice agreeing to disagree about a topic in which neither of you is emotionally invested.

As you listen to your adolescent talk about the experiences of everyday life, practice empathizing with your adolescent's point of view. Don't be overly concerned about being accurate at first; being able to understand empathically another person's experience is a skill that improves with practice.

Make your expectations clear and explicit with regard to the small things of family living, and whenever you have the chance, regardless of how minor the opportunity seems to be, encourage and reinforce your adolescent's striving for independence and individuality.

By practicing the processes of rational parenting in everyday life, you will be prepared to deal with more stressful events when they occur. You will have developed the basic skills of rational parenting, and perhaps even more important, you will have built a relationship in which both you and your adolescent are free to act authentically when a problem is encountered.

But be realistic in your expectations about yourself as well as about your adolescent. No matter how effective your parenting is, your adolescent will inevitably meet some problems and face some difficulties in the process of growing up. There are bound to be emotional ups and downs, disagreements, complaints, and conflicts. Forget about the ideal model of a perfect parent; it is far more important to be genuinely yourself, with your own faults and shortcomings but with the honesty that can be achieved only by being true to yourself.

Don't worry about making mistakes in parenting. As one of our sons told us, to err is parental—so learn to live with and accept your parental humanity.

Although there is no simple formula that guarantees success in human development, by making rational parenting a part of everyday life, you can most effectively help your adolescent through the years of transition to a healthy, happy, and achieving maturity.

Epilogue

Our sons have emerged from adolescence. Now that they are in their early twenties, the luxury of reminiscing about their adolescent years can be done without tensions. Both agreed that at times it was rough and confusing for them as well as for us. They also agreed that there were wonderful moments as they discovered themselves, their own personalities, and began to look at their parents with a bit more realism.

We asked them to tell us the one thing, above all, that they felt made a difference in their lives during that time. Without hesitation, both said that it was the fact that "the door was always open." Despite what they did or what they said, despite the turbulence of the moment, they knew the bottom line was that we cared; we were available to talk and, even more important, listen.

We think their metaphor for our efforts to understand, to make sure the communication lines were never severed, is an apt one. "Keeping the door open" underscores the philosophy of communication and understanding we've tried to convey in this book. It is one thing parents must engrave indelibly on their minds.

As parents, perhaps the best legacy we can hand down to our adolescent children is just this sense of caring and communication—two things so easily forgotten in those few short years when the world turns upside down and spins as adolescents reach out to achieve adulthood.